# Power Of Discovery

For Contractors & Aging-In-Place Providers

*Who, What, When, Where, & More In Creating A Solution*

# Power Of Discovery

## For Contractors & Aging-In-Place Providers

*Who, What, When, Where, & More In Creating A Solution*

### Steve Hoffacker

CAPS, MCSP, MIRM

# Power Of Discovery

## For Contractors & Aging-In-Place Providers

*Who, What, When, Where, & More In Creating A Solution*

ALL RIGHTS RESERVED.

© 2010, 2015 by Hoffacker Associates LLC
West Palm Beach, Florida, USA
ISBN: 978-0-9843524-5-6

Each person who may need and want your remodeling or assessment services as they consider how best to age successfully in their homes has different needs, abilities, interests, requirements, desires, budgets, expectations, and motivations that may not be immediately obvious or apparent when you first meet or talk with them. Therefore, you must ask questions to learn how to help them — and ultimately create an effective solution and structure a sale.

# Other Aging-In-Place & Universal Design Sales Books By Steve Hoffacker

Find additional books (softbound print editions and Kindle eBooks) by Steve Hoffacker on aging-in-place, universal design, and remodeling sales at http://steve hoffacker.com/aginginplacesalesbooks.html):

"**Hitting The Mark:** *The A-B-C's Of Rating Your Aging-In-Place Customers*"

"**Mining Your Database:** *Making More Sales Through People You Already Know*"

"**Filling Your Funnel:** *Building Your Business By Reaching Out To Strangers*"

"**Universal Design For Builders:** *Building & Selling Accessible, Safe & Comfortable New Homes*"

"**Common Sense Universal Design:** *Creating Accessible, Safe, Comfortable & Desirable Homes*"

"**Universal Design And Aging:** *Keeping Our Homes Safe, Accessible & Comfortable As We Age In Place*"

"**Universal Design For Safety:** *Creating Safe & Accessible Living Spaces For All Ages*"

# Table Of Contents

| Chapter | Page |
|---|---|

**Preface** ............................. **13**

**1. Who?** ............................. **19**

    A Straightforward Beginning .............. 19
    Getting Their Name ................... 20
    Writing It Down ..................... 21
    Learning The Correct Spelling ............. 21
    How's That Pronounced? ................ 22
    The Initial Customer Meeting ............. 23
    The Total Customer Unit ................ 24
    The Dynamics Of The Customer Unit ........ 25
    Determining Relationships ............... 26
    Are Others Involved? .................. 27
    Are They Looking For Themselves? .......... 28
    Make A Note Of Everyone ............... 30
    Relationships Can't Be Assumed ........... 31
    Nothing Can Be Assumed ............... 32
    The "Influencers" .................... 33

Selling To The Absent Influencers . . . . . . . . . . 35
Avoiding Surprises With Influencers . . . . . . . . . 36
Assuming There Is Someone Else . . . . . . . . . . . 38
Assuming There Must Be A Family . . . . . . . . . . 39
Identifying The Key Decision-Maker . . . . . . . . . 40
Obtaining Referrals . . . . . . . . . . . . . . . . . . . . . 41
Using Testimonials From Friends . . . . . . . . . . . 42
Tapping Into Current Clients . . . . . . . . . . . . . . 43
Asking About Your Team . . . . . . . . . . . . . . . . 44
Discussing Your Competition . . . . . . . . . . . . . 45
Doing Your Homework . . . . . . . . . . . . . . . . . . 46
More Than Just Introductions . . . . . . . . . . . . . 48
Remember Those Influencers . . . . . . . . . . . . . 49

## 2. What? . . . . . . . . . . . . . . . . . . . . . . . . . . . . . . 51

Opinion, Preference, Or Fact . . . . . . . . . . . . . . 51
What Are They Looking For? . . . . . . . . . . . . . . 52
Getting Started . . . . . . . . . . . . . . . . . . . . . . . . 53
"Breaking The Ice" . . . . . . . . . . . . . . . . . . . . . 54
An Issue Of Communication . . . . . . . . . . . . . . 55
Needing To Ask More Questions . . . . . . . . . . . 56
When People Aren't Expressive . . . . . . . . . . . . 57
Starting With What They Have Now . . . . . . . . . 58
Starting Over With What They Have . . . . . . . . . 59
Mixing Up The Questions . . . . . . . . . . . . . . . . 61
Focusing On Their Interests . . . . . . . . . . . . . . 62
Learning About Their Expectations . . . . . . . . . 63

Getting Onto Their Short List . . . . . . . . . . . . . 65
When The End Comes Too Soon . . . . . . . . . . . . 66
Knowing What You Want To Do Next . . . . . . . . 67
Establishing Common Ground . . . . . . . . . . . . . 68
Learning About Special Conditions . . . . . . . . . . 71
Asking Financial Questions . . . . . . . . . . . . . . . 72
How Realistic Are They? . . . . . . . . . . . . . . . . . 75
Asking The Closing Question . . . . . . . . . . . . . . 75

## 3. When? . . . . . . . . . . . . . . . . . . . . . . . . . . . 77

Future Or Past Events . . . . . . . . . . . . . . . . . 77
Avoid Asking About "Time Frame" . . . . . . . . . 78
It's The Decision Date That Matters . . . . . . . 79
The Fallacy Of "Time Frame" . . . . . . . . . . . . 79
Don't Waste Your Questions . . . . . . . . . . . . . 80
More Information Needed . . . . . . . . . . . . . . . 81
There's No Time Like Today . . . . . . . . . . . . . 81
Learning About Pending Events . . . . . . . . . . 83
Using Related Questions . . . . . . . . . . . . . . . . 83
Determining Future Contact Dates . . . . . . . . 84

## 4. Where? . . . . . . . . . . . . . . . . . . . . . . . . . . . 85

Responses Tend To Be Factual . . . . . . . . . . . . 85
"Where" Questions Are Versatile . . . . . . . . . . . 86
Resources Used To Locate You . . . . . . . . . . . . 86
Determining Preferences . . . . . . . . . . . . . . . . 87
Using "Nesting" . . . . . . . . . . . . . . . . . . . . . . . 87

Personalization . . . . . . . . . . . . . . . . . . . . . . . 88
Making The Decision . . . . . . . . . . . . . . . . . . . 89

## 5. Why? . . . . . . . . . . . . . . . . . . . . . . . . . . . . . . 91

The Most Basic Question . . . . . . . . . . . . . . . . 91
Don't Overuse . . . . . . . . . . . . . . . . . . . . . . . . 91
"Why" — In Other Words . . . . . . . . . . . . . . . . 92
Motivating Influences . . . . . . . . . . . . . . . . . . 93
Experiences In The Marketplace . . . . . . . . . . . 94
Measuring Preferences . . . . . . . . . . . . . . . . . 95
Clarifying Other Issues . . . . . . . . . . . . . . . . . 95
Facilitating The Close . . . . . . . . . . . . . . . . . . 96
Teaming Up With Other Questions . . . . . . . . . 97
Working With Objections . . . . . . . . . . . . . . . . 97

## 6. How? . . . . . . . . . . . . . . . . . . . . . . . . . . . . . . 99

Measuring An Amount Or Opinion . . . . . . . . . . 99
An Introductory Question . . . . . . . . . . . . . . . 100
"How" Leads To Other Questions . . . . . . . . . . 100
Learning About Their Online Search . . . . . . . . 101
Finding Out About Other Sources . . . . . . . . . . 101
Questions Are Interchangeable . . . . . . . . . . . 103
Indicating Preferences And Intent . . . . . . . . . 103
Creating Tie-Downs . . . . . . . . . . . . . . . . . . . 104
Of Degrees And Amounts . . . . . . . . . . . . . . . 105
Measuring With "How Much" . . . . . . . . . . . . . 105
Learning Timing With "How Soon" . . . . . . . . . 105

Table Of Contents 11

    Using "How Long" To Focus . . . . . . . . . . . . . . 106
    Making Direct Comparisons . . . . . . . . . . . . . . 106
    Forming Conclusions . . . . . . . . . . . . . . . . . . 107

**7. Which?** . . . . . . . . . . . . . . . . . . . . . . . . . . **109**

    The Ultimate Choice Question . . . . . . . . . . . . 109
    Don't Force It . . . . . . . . . . . . . . . . . . . . . . . 109
    Reflexive Questions . . . . . . . . . . . . . . . . . . . 110
    Getting Market Information . . . . . . . . . . . . . 111
    Asking The Closing Question . . . . . . . . . . . . . 112
    Setting Up Trial Closes . . . . . . . . . . . . . . . . . 113
    Asking "Which" In Other Ways . . . . . . . . . . . 113

**8. More Questions** . . . . . . . . . . . . . . . . . . . . **115**

    Other Possibilities . . . . . . . . . . . . . . . . . . . . 115
    Yes/No Questions . . . . . . . . . . . . . . . . . . . . 116
    Trial Closing Or Selection Questions . . . . . . . . 117
    Questions That Lead To Another . . . . . . . . . . 118
    Use This Tool Appropriately . . . . . . . . . . . . . 118
    Scaling Questions For Opinions . . . . . . . . . . . 119
    Scaling Question Limitations . . . . . . . . . . . . . 119
    Examples Of Scaling Questions . . . . . . . . . . . 121
    Using Scaling Questions To Clarify . . . . . . . . . 122
    Alternate-Choice Questions . . . . . . . . . . . . . 123
    Getting A Definitive Answer . . . . . . . . . . . . . 125
    Versatility Of This Technique . . . . . . . . . . . . 125
    The Probe . . . . . . . . . . . . . . . . . . . . . . . . . 125

The Porcupine . . . . . . . . . . . . . . . . . . . . . . .126
Answering Objections . . . . . . . . . . . . . . . . . 128
The Troll . . . . . . . . . . . . . . . . . . . . . . . . . . . . 128
Avoid Taking The Bait . . . . . . . . . . . . . . . . . 129

## 9. Go Discover . . . . . . . . . . . . . . . . . . . . . . . . 131

Summary Of Question Choices . . . . . . . . . . . 131
The Inter-Relationship Of Questions . . . . . . . . 132
Keep The Questions Interesting . . . . . . . . . . 133
So Now What? . . . . . . . . . . . . . . . . . . . . . . . 133

# Preface

*Providing aging-in-place solutions for people with various needs – and meeting those individual needs with a customized approach – is a challenging and rewarding pursuit. I applaud you for getting involved in this very important endeavor.*

*Each customer who visits your office, warehouse, store, display, or showroom — or contacts you by phone or email (or even through a friend or relative) — is different.*

*People have various needs, interests, requirements, budgets, preferences, lifestyles, timetables, and abilities to act — and it's up to you to figure out what these are.*

*No one will walk into your office or showroom wearing a sign or handing you a card with their profile on it. The same is true when you visit them at their home.*

*This is true even when there are apparent physical issues present because there can be a lot more going on than just what you see.*

*You will need to conduct a skillful interview with your customers to learn what their needs are and how you can help them. Occupational therapists or skilled consultants can help remodelers and contractors conduct this part of the presentation.*

*Of course, some people will have a more immediate need than others to work with you or obtain the product or solution that you are suggesting.*

*Some will be ready to make a decision on what they want during your initial visit with them, but you will likely work with most people a few times before they feel comfortable in deciding to purchase what you offer.*

*Some will need help sorting through all the various opportunities available to them and determining which company or solution they want to choose.*

*Some people may talk with you several times and never make a commitment to do anything.*

*Others will have a very hard time convincing themselves to make a decision because of the complexity of their needs, requirements, or expectations.*

*So how do you figure out what people are looking for in a new, additional, or replacement design or product and which ones are serious about making a purchase or getting started?*

*Begin by asking appropriate questions in a conversational way and eliciting opinions, likes, dislikes, needs, requirements, preferences, experiences, budget, timing, and impressions.*

*Then you can act on what people tell you and begin to address their needs and start to solve their issues with what you have to offer.*

*"Discovery" is the term for asking a variety of questions to determine someone's needs and ability to act — much like a reporter composing a story.*

*It's what you'll use to get to the "yes" that signifies an agreement on an effective solution for their needs.*

*To get to that point, you'll need to ask a series of questions during your face-to-face presentation with someone to learn the "who," "what," "when," "where," "why," "how," and "which" of what they are seeking as they shop for someone to help them resolve the issues that they are expressing to you.*

*You also can use yes/no questions ("Do you like this color?" or "Is this what you had in mind?") — but often these questions don't give you enough information to work with, and you'll need to ask additional questions anyway.*

*To learn what people really are thinking, you need to get them involved in expressing their opinions and sharing their attitudes with you by asking them questions that go beyond just a short answer.*

*You need for your customers and clients to offer explanations for their opinions and their preferences.*

*When customers reach out to you, they have various needs, requirements, and capacities to make a decision — it's up to you to find out what those are.*

*By asking questions skillfully, you can determine how to help people find what they are seeking — and make more sales in the process.*

*You may be dealing with sensitive issues, or ones involving a lot of emotion or money, and you need to be ready to accept this responsibility.*

*You must skillfully guide them through the many issues and considerations that will affect and impact their decision.*

*This is where knowing how to ask the appropriate questions — and how to ask them in a variety of ways — will make you an effective communicator and an outstanding salesperson.*

*There are many ways of asking the same type of question — or for obtaining similar information — and we'll take a look at some of those in this book.*

*To make a sale and get to the "yes," communication is the key.*

# Power Of Discovery

## For Contractors & Aging-In-Place Providers

---

*Who, What, When, Where, & More In Creating A Solution*

# 1

# Who?

## A Straightforward Beginning

You are in the people business, so when someone visits your location (office, showroom, or offsite display), emails you, or calls for information, the first thing that matters — before you learn anything else about them — is who the person is that has contacted you.

The same is true if you call on them directly although you likely will know the name of the person you are calling or visiting — even if you have never met face-to-face previously.

Nevertheless, you want their name. Then you can begin learning other details.

The "who" question is different than all of the other questions that you'll ask your potential customers and people who might develop into customers you can serve at a later date.

It has nothing to do with their opinions, preferences, wants, needs, expectations, or anything else of a qualitative nature. It doesn't relate to what you can provide.

This type of question calls for a factual response and will yield a specific name or a relationship — or both.

## Getting Their Name

Often, people will introduce themselves when they call you, or you'll have their name on their email or online information request form.

Otherwise, a great way to obtain the name or names of your customers is to offer yours first as you are greeting them and shaking hands with them (or as you are introducing yourself — if it's on the phone or by email).

Many times your customers will reflexively provide their names in response to your introduction. If they don't, it's simple enough to ask for their names at that point.

For instance, when you're shaking hands with your new customers and they don't offer their names when you provide yours, simply hold onto their hand for a moment longer and ask, "*And you are?*" or "*And your name is?*"

Then listen carefully for what they say and repeat it aloud. Be ready with a notepad to record what you hear or what they tell you.

## Writing It Down

Write down everyone's first and last name on your information card or notebook — get in the habit of always carrying something to write on, such as a nice looking folio, and a pen to use.

Be sure to note the correct spelling and pronunciation. If they use a nickname, note it as well. Make sure that you've written it clearly enough to be able to read it again later.

Even if you use a computer, tablet, or smartphone to store your customer records, make a note of the names and other important information on paper first and then transfer them to your database later.

Make sure to obtain the names of everyone present in the customer unit (regardless of age, relationship, title, or authority) so that you can include them — directly and specifically by name — in your presentation and your follow-up contact.

## Learning The Correct Spelling

How will you know if you have the correct spelling of their names? Don't guess. Don't write down what you think they are saying. You need to ask.

Often names sound alike but are spelled quite differently — depending on nationality, ethnicity, or pronunciation.

Take a name that sounds to you like "*Meyer.*" It can also be "*Myer,*" "*Meijer,*" "*Maier,*" "*Mayer,*" "*Majer,*" "*Myers,*" "*Meyers,*" "*Moyers,*" "*Mires,*" "*Miers,*" or "*Meijers.*"

Even a common sounding surname such as "*Johnson*" could also be spelled "*Johnston*" or "*Johnstone*" or "*Jonson*" or "*Jonsen*" — and there are even more variations with first names, depending on nationality, gender, personal preference, and other factors.

Many first names can be used by either men or women. Sometimes they're spelled differently (such as "*Tony,*" or "*Toni,*" or "*Terry,*" or "*Teri*"), and many times they aren't.

Don't rely on what you *think* you hear. Ask.

When someone tells me their name is "*Johnson,*" I ask them: "*Is that with or without the 't'?*" or I ask "*Is that J-o-h-n-s-o-n?*"

## How's That Pronounced?

How will you know if you are pronouncing their first or last names correctly? Or the name of someone who is part of the decision but absent on the initial meeting?

Whether it's the first name or last — or both — you don't want to risk irritating or alienating your customers, or starting off your presentation poorly, by messing up how you say their names.

Begin by repeating each name after you hear it and then immediately write them down, spelled correctly — first and last names.

Your customers either will acknowledge that you have said their names properly or they will politely correct you. They will help you because they want to hear their names said correctly.

After you are sure that you are hearing their names correctly, make notes on your information card, profile form, or notepad as to how to say them properly, and then say their names aloud again (using your notes as a key) — just to make sure that you have it right.

Make all the pronunciation keys or notes that you need on your notepad or card so that you can say their names correctly — long, short, or soft vowel sounds, silent letters, a word that sounds like all or part of how the name is said, accent marks, or anything else that helps you get it right.

They will never see your notes, so don't be bashful about helping yourself to say the names properly — and they will get to hear their names said correctly as a result.

## The Initial Customer Meeting

After you complete the introductions and learn the name or names of your customers — and write them down and know that you are pronouncing each name correctly —

move on to determining the number of people in the customer unit.

It doesn't matter where the presentation or conversation occurs either — your location, theirs, a coffee shop, or at a home show or event — or how many people are present.

It centers on how many people may need to be involved, directly or indirectly, in the decision as well as who the specific individuals are — even if they aren't all present initially or you don't actually ever meet or speak with each one of them. This is *key* to making a sale.

You must know who you are working with and how each person factors into the decision-making process in order for you to be effective and successful. This includes those present as well as ones who will need to be consulted or involved later.

Regardless of how many people you are meeting with or talking to at the time, you ultimately need to determine how many people will be involved in the decision — directly or indirectly.

## The Total Customer Unit

The total customer unit can be a single person, a couple (married or not), a family (nuclear or extended), or more. It can involve relatives, caregivers, consultants, neighbors, social service agencies, financial planners, attorneys, influencers, and others who have a stake in the well-being of the people who are the subject of your renovation or design solution.

A customer unit could be a single person but more than likely is the collective body that will make the decision to acquire or pass on the product, project, or solution you are presenting to them.

In fact, those outside the immediate family or household may carry as much or even more weight in making the final decision than those you meet initially — they may be only part of the total customer unit or the one doing research.

There may be several other people, officially and unofficially, who will factor into the final decision.

It's up to you to determine how large the customer unit is, how it's constituted, and who everyone is that's a member of it. Ask questions. Observe. Take notes. Include all of them in your discussion and consideration.

## The Dynamics Of The Customer Unit

Whether you are selling or providing a renovation, upgrade, reconfiguration, or remodeling project for general purposes or specifically for an aging-in-place need, or you are performing a safety or accessibility assessment, or you are offering a health-related product for the home, you may not initially meet or talk with the person ultimately responsible for the decision – even if they live alone.

There can be a series of influencers – family members, well-meaning neighbors, or professionals – who will guide the decision. Some of them may be the primary financial contributor for the improvements you are suggesting.

In the case of existing or planned multigenerational households where you have the primary adult or adults who head the household, their children (from any age even into their thirties), grandchildren perhaps, parents, in-laws, or other older relatives all living together, you have to appeal to the collective needs and desires in creating a solution.

There could be other relatives (aunts, uncles, cousins, grandparents, adult children, or adult siblings) not living in the home, best friends, neighbors, financial planners, attorneys, social service or senior agencies, support groups, and occupational therapists or other health care professionals who may advise, impact, or influence the decision.

Some of this advice or influence may be volunteered, and some input may be specifically requested by your customer or you.

## Determining Relationships

Ultimately, you need to know who you're working with and how they might be related to each other — if at all. This is true regardless of the size or scope of the remodeling or renovation project.

Some of the people you meet initially or along the way may have no bearing on the final decision, and others who should be present or consulted for their input are not.

Therefore, as you meet your customers and learn who they are, you can observe how people seem to be related to each other and any body language clues that seem to indicate a particular deference to a decision-maker.

Nevertheless, you can't assume anything about anyone's relationship to someone else or family status. You are just forming a picture of who you are working with, how they relate to each other (formally or informally), and ultimately who might be involved in the decision.

## Are Others Involved?

In the case of someone who walks unaccompanied into your showroom, office, facility, or home show booth — depending on whether you have display space and how common it might be for consumers to come to you — you need to determine for yourself if anyone else needs to be included or involved in a potential decision, or if those other individuals (related to this person or not) will be assisting your unaccompanied customer in their decision.

You can ask if anyone else might need to be consulted, if

it is their desire to involve someone else in the decision, or if another person will be a party to the decision, but you shouldn't infer or openly suggest that they can't make the decision on their own. You don't have any basis for making that conclusion or assumption until you clarify the situation.

And, this doesn't apply just to people who contact you. It applies to anyone — regardless of whether it's just one person or several — that want to learn about your products, solutions, or vision for their expressed needs.

It also applies when you go to them. You may encounter just one person or several — even if more are to be involved at a later time in considering your proposal or in making the decision.

## Are They Looking For Themselves?

Begin by asking the person you meet initially if they are looking for something for themselves. Are they the end user of what they will be discussing and evaluating with you, or are they just gathering information?

Regardless of how they answer your question, yes or no in terms of being the decision-maker and the person seeking the solution, you then want to learn if other people might be involved in the decision — or if they plan to consult with others or return with them before making a purchasing decision.

Examples of such questions that you can ask include *"Are you looking for something (a solution) for yourself?"* or *"Are you the one who is going to using <name or description of the design, product, or solution>?* or *"Will this <name or description of your product or the solution you are discussing> be just for you?"* or *"Are you the one who is ultimately going to be making the decision to move forward with your new kitchen (bath, porch, renovation/lighting/flooring/remodeling/redesign) project?"* or *"Are you the one who is going to be making the decision on your remodeling project, or might there be someone else that you will want to bring into the discussion (conversation)?"*

You can also ask *"Will there be someone else (Is anyone else) helping you make a decision on your renovation?"* or *"Is there anyone else involved in helping you make a decision on your <name or description of your product or type of improvement>?"* or *"Are there others you will need to check with before you can go ahead with your decision on <name or description of your product or renovation>?"* or *"Are there other people that you will want to get involved in helping you look at or decide on <name or description of your product or solution>?"*

This does not suggest that someone else will need to be involved or that you assume them to be incapable of a decision on their own. It is simply a confirmation question and an opportunity for you to learn if you are talking with the sole and only decision-maker or influencer.

Whether you are speaking with the person you are meeting with in their home, at your place of business, or at a home show or event, you want to make sure that this person is the one who will be using your product or remodeling or contracting service. Then, you still need to know about other people who may be involved in helping them make the decision — directly or indirectly.

Influencers could include children (either children at home, adult children, or even grandchildren who visit frequently), a fiancé/fiancée, parents, in-laws, siblings, a friend, close neighbors, other relatives, a designer, a financial advisor, an attorney, or a professional such as an OT, PT, or someone else in health care.

## Make A Note Of Everyone

In addition to the names of the people you directly meet initially and note on your information card or notebook, make sure to record the names of other people who are going to be part of the decision as you learn who they are — even if you never actually meet or speak with them.

Again, pay special attention to the way names are spelled and pronounced. Do your best. You won't always have complete information initially.

For instance, it might be a cousin in Cincinnati, a sister in Kansas City, an aunt in Boston, or someone else who is identified more by a description than a specific name.

Also make a note for yourself, and other team members when that is the case, of who the more prominent people are in terms of influence — even if they live in another city or you never speak with them face-to-face.

## Relationships Can't Be Assumed

Relationships aren't always as they seem. You need to clarify who you are working with and identify who the decision-makers are and what contribution they will make to the eventual decision in order to proceed with your presentation effectively.

Even if two people appear to be husband and wife or introduce themselves to you in that way — or you set an appointment to meet with them in their home and verify before your meeting that they are married and joint owners of the property — you can't make any assumptions about family size or anyone else who might be participating in the decision.

Regardless of their age or anything that you see in the home that may suggest that others live there with them, they may or may not be relying on the opinions, advice, or contributions of children, parents, friends, relatives, or other advisors. You just can't make assumptions.

If you meet with two men (or two women) at your office or their home, one of them might be looking for what you are offering with their friend (who is just there to accompany the other one), or they both could be looking for what you offer for individual homes or a home they share — whether they are related or not.

There might be one potential sale between the two of them — with one being the primary decision-maker and the other the advisor. There could be two or more potential sales.

If they are looking to engage you separately for their own particular solutions and simply decided to visit your showroom or home show booth together (or have you visit them), they could be relying upon the help and advice of each other or even additional people who aren't present — that you won't know about without determining this.

Even if they happen to be related in some way, they still might not intend to make a joint purchase.

Then, they could be close friends, neighbors, or even family friends with the unofficial title of aunt or uncle who meet with you — with one of them making the decision for their own particular situation and the other person providing support and counsel.

### Nothing Can Be Assumed

The point is you just don't know how — or if — people are related to each other, how they will make a purchasing decision, how many people will be involved or consulted before arriving at the decision, or what factors might enter into the ultimate decision.

You can't assume anything. Always keep this in mind.

You must ask questions.

The reason you must find out who in your customer unit is making or influencing the purchasing decision — and if there could be additional people present who are interested in having their home renovated as well — is so that you can focus on making your presentation to include the appropriate person or individuals.

This is true whether any or all of these other influential people are present at your initial meeting. In fact, you might not ever meet or speak with them in person. With Skype, Facetime, and other web connections, the ability to talk with someone not present — while actually seeing them during your conversation — is increased.

Don't forget to take into account that there can be people behind the scenes — even living hours away — that you never meet that still have valuable input to help your client decide on what you are offering them.

## The "Influencers"

The "influencers" definitely have to be taken into consideration to build a sale and make it happen. They may not live in your client's home, but their influence will carry a lot of weight in the ultimate decision if your clients rely on their input and advice.

They won't be signing the purchase agreement or scope of services order, but they definitely can impact or influence the decision. They could even have a financial stake in the improvements you are designing or proposing.

You always need to learn who the people are that you are working with directly, but it's essential that you also determine who else will be involved in the decision — directly or indirectly.

Try to learn specifically what it is that the influencers will be adding to the discussion — based on their professional expertise, their fondness for your client or customer, they have gone through a similar remodeling experience, or that they just need to be consulted for their opinion.

Be sure to note who these influencers are and how to contact them so you can keep them apprised of what you are presenting and specifically include them in the decision-making process.

Write their names on your information card on in your notebook, spell their names correctly (ask to make sure you get capture them right), explain or note the relationships (formal or informal) to your customers (and their areas of expertise if there are any), and add any pronunciation keys or other comments that you might need.

To indicate the names of any and all influencers on your card or in your notes, put such names in parentheses — "(*names of missing people*)" — to show you and others who may use your notes that there are such people that are going to factor into the overall decision.

Even if the person is not immediately identified by name but just by relationship — or even if that person is in a different part of the country or not even familiar with your area, note that person anyway the best way that you can ("*co-worker,*" "*friends from the office,*" or "*cousin in Chicago*").

## Selling To The Absent Influencers

If your potential customers or clients mention other people who will be influencing their decision, be sure to include these other people in your presentation or conversation, using their names or relationships as you refer to them.

Make certain to specifically seek the approval of those influencers or decision-makers who are not present.

Ask your customers how well they think that their absent influencers might like something that you are showing them (such as colors, styles, finishes, or design concepts), or if they think that their influencers might want you to go in a different direction and look at another type of product or solution.

For instance, you might ask *"Is this the kind (type) of product (solution, design) you think your cousin Bill (other influencer) would approve of (like, desire, want) for you?"* or *"Is this the kind (type) of product (solution) you think your sister Eileen has in mind for you?"*

*"What do you think your parents (children, brother, financial advisor, sister, for instance) would say about our approach to your issues?"* or *"Do you think that your uncle (cousin, other influencer) would consider us to be on the right track with what I'm showing you?"* or *"Have you talked with your brother Tom (sister, other influencer) about what we've discussed so far about my (our) proposal for solving your concerns?"*

There are several other question possibilities for learning what someone who needs to be consulted might feel about what you are discussing or the way in which you are evaluating what you feel needs to be done — including the specific design approach, safety concerns, priorities, and the budget.

## Avoiding Surprises With Influencers

Imagine working with someone for several minutes — or even for more than one meeting or conversation — and thinking that you are getting close to reaching an agreement on a design, product, or solution for them when they mention that they need to discuss the whole issue of getting started or moving forward with someone else. Maybe you even question how serious they are about doing something.

They allow you to believe or act as if they're in control of the buying process as they reflect on or seem quite interested in what you're showing or discussing with them, but they wait until well along in the conversation or your presentation — possibly the very end of it — to mention the other person or people.

This could be a legitimate need to involve others, or it could be a big smokescreen designed to deflect the need to make a decision.

Nevertheless, until that moment, you didn't realize that anyone else (identified or not) was going to be a factor in the buying process.

Wouldn't it have been nice to know about this other person or persons at the outset and that they would somehow factor into the decision? And what about the expertise or viewpoint that they supposedly could contribute to the conversation or ultimate decision?

Had you known, you could have tailored your presentation toward appealing to those people that might participate in, comment on, or affect the decision — and not have assumed that you were talking with the sole decision-maker or makers.

This is why discovery questions about people participating in the discussion or decision to acquire a product or solution such as you are offering are so necessary.

Sometimes people will tell you that there is no one else involved in the decision and then later say that they need to check with someone or talk to them as a way of buffering or diffusing your pursuit of the sale or order. How ready they are to decide might be a factor also.

However, if you ask about other people early in your presentation, customers often will reveal the names or relationships of other people that will be part of the decision — particularly if they think that this will take the pressure off them so they can just look at or listen to what you are presenting.

## Assuming There Is Someone Else

Never assume anything about someone's level of authority, or their ability to make a decision. You must get clarification. Misreading the situation could easily cost you an appointment, sale, or referral.

A person unaccompanied by anyone else — who truly is acting alone — that you assume must have a partner, spouse, or family will likely be quite offended and turned off by the implication or suggestion that they are not capable of a decision on their own or that they need the help of someone else to make a decision.

This means that making a sale or getting an appointment to visit their home to present possible solutions is probably not very likely due to the way they were treated.

## Assuming There Must Be A Family

Rather than a single person or one unaccompanied by someone else, you may have couples shopping in your showroom or allowing you to set an appointment to meet with them in their home. You still need to be careful with appearances.

A man and woman may arrive at your location together and have children with them — particularly younger children. You might find a similar situation when you visit their home. Older individuals may have their adult children or grandchildren with them.

It may appear to be a family, but you cannot immediately assume that it is. You need to clarify who is present and how each of them factors into a decision that you want to achieve. Typically, it would be a husband and wife with their own children, but it could other situations as well.

It could be an unmarried couple with their own children.

Then again, the children could belong to either the man or the woman, or some to each of them.

It also could be a husband and wife or unmarried couple with some of their own children and some of their children's friends or cousins.

The children could be other relatives of the adults, such as nieces, nephews, or grandchildren. This could be true even if the adults you are working with have other children — present with them or not.

## Identifying The Key Decision-Maker

Whether there are absent influencers or not, you also need to know who in your customer unit is the most influential or prominent decision-maker. There will be just one.

This is true whether it is a medically necessary improvement or one for other reasons such as an update for safety or newer technology.

You must receive the approval from the key decision-maker in order to actually make the sale or obtain the appointment to proceed further. It might even be someone outside the immediate household such as a caregiver, medical professional, or relative.

This person may lead the discussion or take a less vocal

posture. In fact, he or she might not even be present at some of the meetings, appointments, or conversations you have — including the initial visit.

Nevertheless, this is the person who ultimately will make the decision for your product, service, design, or solution.

As you are conducting your discovery and learning about your customers, you need to determine who the person is in the customer unit that you need to secure the "yes" from to signify an ownership decision.

This is the person you need to appeal to and make sure that they are comfortable with what you are offering — even if they are not present at the initial meeting or even if they are not the chief beneficiary of your remodeling solution or assessment.

You must secure the support, approval, and agreement of the primary decision-maker in order to make a sale. Keep in mind that the key decision-maker may not be the one who is financing the purchase.

## Obtaining Referrals

Securing referrals is a large part of producing additional customers and capitalizing on your sales lead generation and advertising investment. It costs absolutely nothing for you to ask for a referral, and your customers are going to know people that you don't.

If you don't learn about other people through your customers, you won't have the opportunity to contact and connect with them about what you offer. Your customers will reflect on the wonderful service and solutions you are providing as they think of people to recommend.

Even when people have decided that they want to work with another company — or you determine that they are not in a position to make a decision in the near future — the people you have invested a little time in getting to know still might be aware of people that should talk with you or hear about your services. So ask. This is an important part of building your business. Don't miss it.

## Using Testimonials From Friends

Another type of referral and a great "who" question that you can ask people during your discovery process is who they might know that already has worked with you or looked at some of your products, designs, or services.

If they have been referred to you by a professional resource or a previous customer, make sure to explore why they are looking forward to working with you. This will go a long way in making the sale.

You'll want to learn what their friends, relatives, or others may have told them that prompted or influenced them to contact you about setting up a meeting to discuss your proposed solutions for their home.

In some cases, you'll already have a good idea of how someone was referred to you and what they are looking for because their friend, neighbor, family member, case worker, or health care professional will have made the initial contact with you to discuss the improvements and make the appointment.

Then, you'll want to reinforce this introduction by discussing with your potential clients what they have been told and how they are looking forward to working you.

Perhaps people have been to your website before contacting you and have a comfort level this way.

Sometimes they may have some familiarity with your company or how you work because they might have accompanied their friends or relatives at an earlier time when they were visiting your showroom or home show booth.

It's possible they have seen your vehicles at job sites or about town or that they have seen some of your advertisements. This is a type of indirect referral where they are associating your visibility in the market with someone that they have a comfort level with already.

### Tapping Into Current Clients

A similar "who" question for your customers is who they know that currently has a home that you restyled, remodeled, reconfigured, or redesigned for their comfort, convenience, safety, or accessibility — whether it was a medically inspired improvement or not.

They have actually been in that home or more than one home, or they know people that you have served and have discussed what you have been able to accomplish for them.

These are very strong referrals.

It's one thing to advertise, to have a website, or to talk with someone about what you can offer. It's quite another for them to actually know and speak with someone who has used your services directly.

In fact, that might be the reason they have reached out to you for the project they are contemplating.

You'll also want to know the nature of the relationship that exists between them and the people you have worked with and how this might have predisposed them to want to begin working with you.

### Asking About Your Team

Another "who" question that might come up in conversation is who they know that works for or with your company — employees, associates, subcontractors, or strategic partners (architects, occupational or physical therapists, designers, and others) — currently or in the past.

Then you can find out what those people might have shared with them about their experiences in working with your company or how they think your company compares to the competition.

## Discussing Your Competition

Still another important "who" question involves your competition and the marketplace.

Get in the practice of asking your customers who else they are familiar with or who they have talked with or know about that can provide a solution such as you are proposing — and if they still intend or think they need to speak to another company before making a decision (and why that is the case).

Have they already met or spoken with someone from a competing company? What have been their experiences?

Learn how what they've encountered in the marketplace compares to what you have been showing or discussing with them. Determine what you might be able to do to compete more favorably with other companies.

Finding out about your competition and your marketplace from your customers is one of the ways to achieve a return on your advertising and lead generation investment — even when no sale or additional activity ever results from the people sharing this information with you.

Make it a practice to ask everyone that you contact or meet with about what you offer what their general experiences have been in the marketplace.

Learn how what they have seen or heard from doing their research compares or contrasts to what you offer and your ability to provide what they are looking for and capacity to be responsive to their specific needs.

Are their expectations realistic? If not, how did they form them and how can you relate to them?

**Doing Your Homework**

In addition to asking your customers about their experiences in the marketplace and who else they might know of or might have talked with about obtaining a product or solution such as you offer, you should do your own homework to examine your marketplace.

You need to take an in-depth look at your market, service area, or territory to determine first-hand who is competing for your customers.

You might belong to a professional organization (local chapters of HBA, NARI, AGC, AOTA, APTA, ASID, IIDA, AIA, or similar professional associations) where you will know others in your group who are vying for business in the areas you serve.

There might be other CAPS designation holders in your area also.

Even if people or businesses that provide similar services as you are not members of a professional organization, you need to know who they are and what types of services they provide.

As you look for and identify competing companies in your service area, determine what they offer and their general market emphasis. There may be great similarity with what you do, or it could be distinctly different.

Search their websites and be aware of articles and posts that might appear in social media or blogs. Do organic keyword searches to find companies you might be unaware of, and pay attention to direct mail and print advertising that your competition is doing. Determine where they might have memberships that your potential customers might regard as beneficial.

Watch for vehicles and job signs of other contractors in areas you serve.

Look at event sponsorships or other types of advertising also from companies that might be competing with you.

Examine your unique selling proposition ("USP") in light of what your competition is presenting to the marketplace and potential consumers.

A "lost sale" (a presentation that you made that did not result in a sale or one that you did not know about until after the decision had been made) is an opportunity to learn about your competition also. It's not a pleasant way of doing so, because someone else got to your potential customer or sales lead before you did.

However, you can learn about who the other company is, what they offer, why this appealed to the person that bought from them, and if there was anything you could or should have done to have earned that sale. It could be price, or it could something else.

Just be aware of the many opportunities to learn about who your competition is so you can focus on staying a step ahead of them or offering something they don't (in terms of a solution, price point, response time, warranty, or other attractive feature).

### More Than Just Introductions

There are plenty of "who" questions that you should ask about and then determine the answers to as you begin developing a relationship with a potential customer and then starting your presentation or dialog with them — regardless of where or how that occurs.

These will guide your discussion and help you get to know the wants, needs, abilities, timing, and seriousness of your customers or potential clients.

Again, not everything you ask needs to include the word "who" in the question — but your customers need to understand that this is the type of information you need and supply it in their responses to you.

Asking "who" questions is much more than just learning the names of people who are present with you.

As we have discussed, learning who people are and how to pronounce their names correctly is very important, but it's only the first step. The same holds true for people that you are "meeting" by telephone and email.

You start by learning the names of anyone who walks into your sales office or showroom, visits your show display, or contacts you by telephone or email.

Then you move on to the many other important "who" issues and questions that you will use to build relationships and ultimately make sales.

## Remember Those Influencers

Don't forget the importance of the influencers — especially the ones who aren't present. Learn who they are so that you can include them by direct reference in your presentation and explore their opinions and comments.

Be mindful of the tremendous impact that friends, relatives, advisors, other health care professionals (besides you or the ones on your team), associates, consultants, influencers, and others can have on the eventual decision, and work to understand how to win their approval.

Remember that the most important influencer of all in making the decision is going to be the major decision-maker in the customer unit.

You must identify this person and specifically sell to him or her.

## 2

# What?

## Opinion, Preference, Or Fact

Asking or using a "what" question seems so basic — and it is.

That's because it can express an opinion, preference, or a fact — as in *"What do you think?"* or *"What is important to you?"* (opinion), *"What color do you prefer?"* or *"What shade of green do you think you would like?"* (preference), or *"What would you like to accomplish?"* or *"What do you use now?"* (fact).

As you meet your customers for the first time — in person, over the telephone, or online — and you begin to learn a little about them, of course you'll want to know who you are talking to. That was the subject of the previous chapter.

Getting their names and learning more about who they are is quite important — along with determining who the chief decision-maker is and any key influencers that need to be consulted or factored into the decision.

## What Are They Looking For?

Along with gathering and learning about "who" in its many forms, you'll need to know what people want, and what it will take to sell them what you offer.

You'll also want to know what they want to accomplish in the renovation project (safety, accessibility, mobility, visitability, comfort, or other important objectives) and what features, colors, styles, and finishes they desire.

You'll need to find out what you are replacing (flooring, appliances, lighting, doors, windows, cabinetry, walls, or more) and what about the current situation is no longer satisfactory for their safety, security, or enjoyment of their living space.

Find out what it is about what they have now that needs changed, replaced, or modified, such as widening the hallway, enlarging or modifying a doorway, adding storage, eliminating steps, enhancing the usefulness of the bathroom, or accommodating someone with special needs.

It could be using new technology for locks or monitoring, better lighting or more of it, easier to use fixtures and controls, or enhanced safety features.

## Getting Started

There are many ways to ask people what they're looking for in a product, design, or solution.

To get the "what" process started, you might begin by asking a general introductory question, such as *"What issues are you looking to resolve?"* or *"What is the main reason we are here?"* or *"What type of a solution are you looking for?"* or *"What are you looking for today?"* or *"What did (do) you have in mind that I can help you with?"* or *"What would you like for me to be able to do for you to resolve your concerns?"*

You can use a statement, such as *"Tell me about what you're looking for,"* or *"Tell me how I can help you,"* or *"Tell me about your concerns (needs, issues),"* or *"Describe what you have in mind for your kitchen (bath, entrance, kitchen, hallway, porch, bedroom),"* or *"Tell me (Describe) what you're thinking about doing in this room"* or *"Tell me about the type of solution you're looking for"* or *"Can you tell me a little bit about what you're looking for in terms of size, features and price range (budget)?"* or *"What would you like to be able to do in this space (area) that you can't do (aren't able to do) right now?"*

## "Breaking The Ice"

This first "what" question is a very simple introductory one. It's asked as much to break-the-ice (like a *"how are you?"* question does) as it is to get a definitive answer from your customers.

While you'd like to learn the specific type of concern they have for their update, modernization, safety makeover, or remodeling project, you may only get a non-focused response when you ask this question.

Some people have a more definite idea of what they want, need, require, or are looking for (in terms of budget, features, and scope). Some only know what they don't want or like.

They may say something like *"We're not really sure,"* or *"We don't know, we just decided to start looking at our options,"* or *"It's kind of early in the process so we don't really know yet,"* or *"We really don't know what's available,"* or *"We're just in the talking stage,"* or *"We're real preliminary at this point,"* or *"We're trying to figure out what our options (choices) are,"* or *"We're not really sure how much we should undertake at this time"* or *"We know what isn't working but we're not sure how to approach it or how much we can do,"* or *"We'd like to make some changes but don't know how much it will cost to do them."*

They may just say that they are looking for something newer, more efficient, cost-effective, sustainable, safer, convenient, accessible, or appealing than they have now that will meet or accommodate their needs — without elaborating — regardless of what they have now. Of course, with traumatic conditions, the need and the solution with be more pressing and better identified.

## An Issue Of Communication

Asking people *"What are you looking for?"* or *"What would you like to have done?"* may seem like a basic question that can be answered relatively easily. However, that's only true if they have thought this through completely or spent some time reviewing their options.

It seems like a factual response could be given, but we know that some people have trouble visualizing or verbalizing what they want — even with the help of others.

Sometimes, people will have a general idea of what they want done or how something needs to change from the way it is now without having a clear idea of what they need, what is involved in doing it, and how much it might cost.

It might be a simple matter of budget, regardless of what is needed or suggested, and it often isn't so much what you think you are asking in this early discovery question.

While you just want a rather simple, straightforward, well-defined answer, you often get just a partial or incomplete answer. You may need to ask several additional questions before you get enough information to have more than just a generalized idea of what they want or what they need to solve the issues they are facing.

Be patient and help them verbalize what they have in mind — even if they initially think that they can't express it. Occupational or physical therapists will be helpful in interpreting this or drawing it out of your customers.

## Needing To Ask More Questions

Instead of a general *"what are you looking for?"* or *"what do you have in mind?"* or *"what do you need done?"* question, you may need to ask a more direct question.

For instance, *"What are you looking to accomplish in remodeling (redesigning, refreshing, reconfiguring) your kitchen (bath or other room or living space)?"* or *"What specifically are you looking for in a solution for this room (area)?"* or *"What issues are you facing that you want (need) to resolve to make your kitchen (bath, entrance, or other space) safer or more useable (accessible)?"* or *"What would you like your kitchen (bath or other area) to look like when we are all finished (done) with your remodel (new look)?"*

Or you might ask *"What specific features are you looking for in your new kitchen (kitchen makeover)?"* or *"What features are important for you to have in your new (reconfigured) kitchen (bath, kitchen makeover)?"* or *"What specifically do you have in mind?"* or *"What ideas* do you have for accomplishing what you are describing to me?" or "What isn't working for you in your home right now?"

You could ask them to *"Describe what type of a look are you trying to achieve (looking for, have in mind)?"*

Other questions are *"Have you seen anything on a TV show, in a magazine, online, or anyplace else that is close to what you're looking for?"* or *"What have you seen anywhere — perhaps online or in a magazine or brochure — that is close to what you're looking for?"* or *"Has anyone suggested what you should have in this space or what it should look like when we are done?"*

## When People Aren't Expressive

Sometimes people just know that they would like to change something (or maybe several things) from what they have now. They might want to add something to what they have now without knowing exactly where to begin. They may know that what they have now just isn't working for them. They may know that it's difficult for some members of the household to use everything in the home.

However, some will be vague intentionally about what they want because they are more interested in looking around and having you show and discuss products or possible solutions for their space or their expressed needs and concerns than they are in actually purchasing something or talking with you in any meaningful way about eventually creating and accomplishing a solution.

Other times, they may have an idea of what they want — or maybe a better idea of what they *don't* want — but they just are having trouble putting it into words. Again, others on your team such as occupational therapists can be helpful here.

You may need to use their current situation for reference — to help them describe or show you what works, what doesn't work, where there are issues or concerns, and what they would like to change or what needs to be different than it is.

## Starting With What They Have Now

Here, skillful questioning is important as you ask about their current situation, how they use their space, and what is working or not working to their satisfaction.

You don't want to put them on the defensive or give them the impression that you are ridiculing or minimizing what they have now. Don't ask them to defend why they chose their current home or anything to do with the layout, colors, furniture, appliances, or finishes. Just learn their likes and dislikes to give you some direction in helping them select a solution for their needs. It could well be that the choices were made before physical limitations were a factor or concern.

Determine what features are important — *"What features in your present layout (this space, kitchen, space, bath) are the most important to you?"* — and what features they use the most or find the most helpful or beneficial. Which ones would they like to replace if they could — regardless of how feasible or expensive it might be to actually accomplish this.

## Starting Over With What They Have

Ask your customers *"If you could redesign (reconfigure, change, restyle) what you're using right now to make it more ideal (desirable, efficient, comfortable, safe, accessible) for your current situation (needs, lifestyle, workflow, output), what would you do (do differently)?"* or *"If you could change anything about your current situation, what would you do?"* or *"What can I do to help you use your kitchen (bath, living space, patio, porch, basement, bedroom) better or enjoy it more?"*

You can ask *"What features are missing from your current layout (kitchen, space, bath, bedroom, porch, laundry room, garage) that you think would make your lives more comfortable or easier?"* or *"What features do you like in your current layout that you definitely want to have included in your next (new) one (your redesign)?"*

The converse of this would be *"What features in your present kitchen (or other room or area) are not that important (functional) to you now?"* or *"What features in* your current kitchen (or other space) would you just as soon not have in your new (next) design (layout, space)?"

Similarly, you can ask "*What aspects of your current situation (design, layout, space) do you want to maintain (retain) as we move forward?*" or "*If you could start over by designing a brand new kitchen (living space) for yourselves, what features would you include in it, what would it need to do or provide, and what would it look like?*"

Obviously, this is the point. They are preparing to start over with a new, upgraded, reconfigured, or remodeled space so this line of questioning can be very revealing in terms of what's important to them and what areas you need to focus on to make a sale. If there are medically necessary features that need to be included, your OT consultant will advise you or take the lead role.

This type of questioning really gets your customers involved in the discussion and is especially helpful when people seem to have difficulty in describing or verbalizing what they're looking for in a solution to their needs.

If it's a major remodel or an addition to the existing space, does the current zoning for that neighborhood — or the community or homeowner regulations — permit such activity? Can what your client or customer (or their influencers) needs to have done be accommodated without applying for variances or changes?

If the current location of the rooms in question are such that the floor space will need to borrow space from adjacent rooms — or be transferred or exchanged with another area in the home — is there sufficient access and space to do this within the physical constraints (footprint) of the structure?

## Mixing Up The Questions

To learn about the "what" aspects of helping people to decide on an appropriate product, feature, design, or solution for them, you don't necessarily have to use the specific word "what" in your questions. The questions just need to be formed in such a way that they will yield these types of responses and tell you what people are seeking, desiring, wanting, or requiring.

Sometimes the word "what" will appear in your questions, but the questions may not begin with that word or even include it in the phrasing — this way you'll provide some variety to your "what" questions.

For instance, you might ask *"Are you looking for …?"* or *"How important is …?"* or *"Is that what you are looking for?"* or *"Is that the kind of feature (design, solution) you are looking for?"* or *"Is that what you are interested in?"* or *"Is this what you have (had) in mind?"*

While a certain amount of *"yes"* and *"no"* questions may be helpful — particularly for people with cognitive challenges — you run the risk of not getting enough information to proceed.

You want questions that will give you a direct "what" response — or help you clarify what your customers are looking for or find important — as you continue to have a conversation with them. Those answered "not sure" or "don't know" aren't helpful.

You could also ask them to *"Describe what you are looking for,"* or *"Tell me what you have in mind,"* or *"Explain what you are wanting (would like) to achieve,"* or *"Describe what's going on in this space that isn't working for you."*

Again, people with cognitive issues will be challenged by this and you will need to employ a different type of questioning or get help from others in the customer unit.

## Focusing On Their Interests

Sometimes people will visit your showroom, office, or show display without a clear idea of what they want or what you offer.

Sometimes they may have an idea of their budget or price range, but not necessarily what they can get for that or how well it will address their needs. Conversely, they may not have a clear idea of how much they will need to spend to get what they have in mind.

They may have seen some ideas on TV programs, online, or in magazines, so you might ask them *"What treatments (brands, designs, components, solutions) have you been focusing on (looking at, considering, exploring)?"* or *"What have you seen so far online, in a magazine, or in someone's home that appeals to you?"* or *"What types (styles) of kitchens (baths, room additions, porches, basements, decks, patios, bedrooms) seem to be on your radar screen right now?"*

You also can ask *"Have you seen or identified anything yet that is close to what you are looking for?"* or *"What have you seen so far anywhere that is close to what you are looking for?"*

*"What is the main thing you are trying to achieve in your renovation?"* or *"What have you visualized (thought about, considered, pictured) as the finished look when we are done?"* or *"What are you looking forward to the most by having us remodel your space?"* can be revealing questions. Of course, asking about their concerns might be helpful also.

## Learning About Their Expectations

"What" questions are great for learning about the expectations of your customers so that you can adapt your discussion to address their needs and interests — and determine what to highlight or focus on in your presentation.

Ask questions such as *"What would you like to accomplish today?"* or *"How much would you like to accomplish today?"* or *"What are you prepared to get done today?"* or *"In our limited time together today, what would you like to accomplish (focus on)?"* or *"What would you like to work on (address) first?"* or *"Where shall we begin?"*

Other questions are *"How can I use your time the most effectively today?"* or *"What are you most interested in seeing or learning about today?"* or *"What is the most important thing for you to see or find out about (learn about) today?"*

Determine if they are just considering their options and gathering information, or are they ready to seriously pursue a solution for their needs — and choose a product or design, as well as a provider, and actually sign a design/build agreement, tender an initial deposit, or make it clear they are ready to proceed by having you prepare a formal scope of services proposal?

You also need to consider and actually ask yourself the same type of question about what you want to accomplish during your time with them — such as general fact-finding, letting them get to know you, presenting possible solutions, or getting a commitment to move forward.

This is true regardless of whether this is a minor or major remodel and if it's being done for general enjoyment of the space or for a specific physical need.

## Getting Onto Their Short List

If it's the first time that you are meeting with or talking to your customers or potential clients about their needs and what you can offer to address those requirements, at a minimum you need to present a strong case as to why you and your company should be a finalist — in the top 2 or 3 — as the one they will select to provide what they are shopping and looking for. This is the "what" that you need to accomplish.

Even if your customers won't admit it, they are taking stock of you, your company, and what you offer to determine if they want to do business with you. You might be the only one being considered at this point, or you could be in competition with several others. Much will depend on the kind of impression you make.

Of course, being recommended or referred to them by an occupational or physical therapist, a case manager, a designer, or other professional that they trust can go a long way in establishing instant credibility. Strategic relationships are essential.

Thus, your primary objective during your initial presentation with someone is to convince them that you are worthy of doing business with them. This is the all-important *"justification"* phase of your overall sales process, and this is what I term *"making it onto their short list."*

If this is a subsequent visit or conversation, you are that much closer to being their selected provider and should determine exactly what remains to be accomplished before that can happen.

Many decisions happen after the initial conversation or visit, and that won't be possible unless you make it onto their short list and then remain on it as they narrow their choices.

## When The End Comes Too Soon

You certainly want to make a significant impression on your customers and their influencers about the abilities and reputation of you and your company (and the strategic partners you might be using) so that you can make it onto their short list and persuade them that you're worthy of remaining as a finalist in their search for a remodeler or aging-in-place service provider.

However, sometimes you may not get an opportunity to present your case completely — or determine what your customers need to see or accomplish. Your presentation may not be able to be completed from start to finish as you had planned.

You may be only partially into your presentation or just started with what you want to show your customers or discuss with them when they need to stop — for a variety of reasons.

Your customers might have a time constraint that they bring up after you get started (that wasn't mentioned previously), or something could come up (even a minor health issue) that brings a hasty and premature end to your presentation.

Thus, as you move along through your presentation, you need to constantly assess what you have accomplished with each customer to that point (during that particular presentation and historically — if this is not the initial conversation) and what needs to happen next.

This is especially important for those times when your presentation ends abruptly before you reach a normal stopping point or conclusion. You must determine what remains to be done, discussed, or shown — and then convey that to your customer.

### Knowing What You Want To Do Next

What do you do in these "hurry-up" cases, and what do you recommend to your customers in each instance as the next step of activity? What do you still need to accomplish with each customer? Make sure you have a plan of how to approach these situations when they arise.

Even when your presentation ends normally with all that you had planned to discuss with them or show them on that visit — or you had covered everything that was feasible for that visit — what remains to be done?

What do you want to do next? What will it take for them to make a decision? What is the most feasible course of action to pursue, based on what has transpired so far and where they are in their decision-making process? What steps have you or should you suggest to them or spell out that need to be accomplished?

These are powerful "what" questions that you need to be ready to answer to be in control of your sales process.

You need to rehearse and prepare for these scenarios so that you have ready answers and suggestions for these questions when they occur — and you need to know how to make such a quick assessment for each customer to keep them involved with you until the next conversation.

## Establishing Common Ground

As you begin working with your customers, you'll want to establish some common ground so that you will have something to talk about during the presentation and during the project if you are selected for it. This adds a human dimension to your business and helps you relate to your customers on a more personal level.

Sometimes, you will have been briefed on hobbies or other interests that your customers have by the strategic partner who referred you. Otherwise, be ready to determine some personal insights about your customers that will provide you with something to talk about with them and guide your designs also.

People like discussing personal experiences or talking about themselves, and if you can speak their language as it relates their profession or hobby, you will help them feel more at ease and be likeable in their eyes as well.

Many times, you just have to ask a good question and then just listen as they share a wealth of information about their experiences, likes, dislikes, history, needs, and requirements.

Depending on the ages and life experiences of your customers, they may have plenty to share with you.

You also can relate to them that some of your past clients or family members are similarly employed (or used to be before they retired if that is the case), that they enjoy similar hobbies and activities, or that you or they have children of that age.

If your children are grown, you can relate what you remember about your children and their activities at that age.

Depending on the ages, family situation, and any special needs that characterize your customers, there could be children present (school age or teen-agers) or just adults — possibly just seniors.

Therefore, be ready to discuss subjects that involve children such as school subjects and activities, sports, hobbies, interests, and other activities that they might be involved in, as well as subjects more suited to their parents or grandparents.

You can ask any children or grandchildren that might be present *"What school do you go to (attend)?"* or *"What grade are you in (going into)?"* or *"What kinds of activities are you in at school?"* or *"Do you play sports?"* or *"What subjects do you enjoy?"* or *"Do you play a musical instrument?"* or *"What college are you planning on attending?"* or *"What do you plan on (are you) majoring in at college?"* or *"What would you like to do (plan on doing) when you graduate?"* or *"What do you like to do when you're not in school?"*

For the adults, you can ask about hobbies, interests, and present or past occupations (if they are retired). These help you connect with your customers and have something more to discuss than just the solutions they are looking for — and it may give you some additional insight into how they process information or approach decisions that you can use in presenting your solutions.

If there are obvious medical issues involved, use your occupational or physical therapist consultant to advise you of how to proceed or provide information you will need so you won't need to ask sensitive or delicate questions.

## Learning About Special Conditions

There might be special issues in the lives of your customers that need to be resolved before they can make a decision on remodeling their space.

These could be family (personal) or economic (financial) issues that mitigate the ability of your customers to focus on reaching a decision or seriously considering what you are showing or presenting to them.

There could also be a disagreement or mini-power struggle among family members or influencers on what improvements are necessary, required, prudent, or financially viable. You should use "what" questions to learn about and explore them.

For instance, there may be long-term medical conditions, an unexpected death in the family, a recent cancer or progressive illness diagnosis, pending or recent surgery, an immobilizing injury, a recent hospital or nursing home stay, or an acute illness that might affect someone's timing or ability to make a decision. Also, the person who is likely to benefit the most from the improvements might be challenged by others to consider other options or incorporate the needs of other persons in the household as well.

Of course, these concerns might be the very reason you are there to present a solution. Accommodating special physical conditions and limitations is a big reason for requesting remodeling and aging-in-place solutions.

Rely on the occupational therapist you have selected to work with to observe what is going on in the home and provide their observations. If your customers have an occupational or physical therapist they already are working with, get that person involved in creating a solution. Even so, use the input of your consultant also.

OTs are skilled at knowing what questions to ask to learn about what is going on in someone's life and to be able to review medical records (when they are authorized by the client to do so) to interpret someone's medical needs and suggest courses of action to meet those needs and provide safe, accessible, and suitable solutions.

There might be financial issues, medical concerns, or both, that need to be resolved or taken into consideration as you plan for remodeling or renovation solutions and improvements.

## Asking Financial Questions

A huge "what" question — and one that is frequently overlooked or ignored — is the one about money and what people can afford to invest in your solution.

Begin with a budget — and determine it as soon as you can. See if you can accomplish this at the first meeting or even during a phone discussion prior to the initial meeting. It governs the renovation process.

Learn what your customer can invest in the improvements they are contemplating or that you might suggest. Have they even thought of or considered how much money it will take to do what they require or envision?

This is where you need to help them come to terms with the total project expenditure — and assist them in prioritizing the work elements in case some things fall outside of a comfortable or workable budget.

They may have just identified a need without giving much consideration to what it will cost to achieve an effective solution and where that money might come from.

There is a tendency to think that asking financial questions about what people can afford or how they intend to pay for the project is somehow improper or "off-limits" and that only a lender or financial officer can go here.

However, you need a general idea of what someone can afford and an awareness of whether they have considered how they are going to pay for the work they need.

If they are going to be applying for a home improvement loan, a second mortgage, or a re-finance, what is their general credit-worthiness for them getting approved for the project? Of course a home equity loan or line-of-credit that they already have will not require any approval or underwriting if they have a sufficient credit limit on their account.

There are many other financing options that might come into play besides a bank loan, such as their savings, financial contributions of family members, life insurance policy loans, worker's comp or liability settlements, health insurance plans, government grants (including the VA), asset liquidation, or contributions from non-profit agencies or support groups.

Begin with the investment amount. *"What are you thinking of investing in your new remodeling (redesign, kitchen project)?"* or *"Do you have an amount that you are trying to stay within as far as the total investment in your new kitchen (bath, porch, patio, family room, basement, garage)?"* or *"What had you thought about as far as what you are willing or able to invest in your new kitchen (bath, porch, patio, family room, basement, garage)?"*

*"What have you budgeted for your new kitchen (bath, porch, patio, family room, basement, garage)"* or *"What amount is comfortable for you to invest in your new kitchen (other improvement)?"* or *"Have you considered what you can afford to do a new kitchen (bathroom remodel, first floor bedroom, elevator)?"* can also be asked.

You might also have to ask something such as *"Do you have an idea of what a new kitchen (kitchen remodel, new entrance, new shower) might cost?"* or *"Do you have a* rough idea of what it will take financially to accomplish your project?" or "What is the upper limit of what you're comfortable investing in what we are talking about?"

### How Realistic Are They?

People simply may not know what they can afford or what it will take to formulate a realistic budget for the work they need or want done.

Whatever amount they say that they are considering investing in their remodeling solutions that you are discussing with them, learn how they determined their projected budget amount or how they arrived at that figure. What is the basis for choosing that number?

They may just be picking a number because it sounds nice compared to what they have now, they saw something in that price range that appealed to them, they got this idea from a TV program, they have done some comparative shopping online, they have gotten other bids or estimates, or a friend, relative, or neighbor had a kitchen remodel in this price range a few years ago.

### Asking The Closing Question

"What" questions help you learn about the needs and interests of your customers. They help you determine what to show or suggest as a way of addressing their needs and concerns.

Sometimes your OT or designer will be able to apprise you of generally what needs to be done, and you can confirm that with your observations and questions.

After you've made your presentation and answered their questions — and received agreement that what you are offering will work for them and fit their budget and timetable — "what" questions can also be used as a final closing question to get the paperwork started.

Ask *"What would you say about getting started today?"* or *"What about making a decision on your new kitchen (bath, patio, basement) while you're (I'm) here?"* or *"What other questions do you have before we get started with the paperwork?"* or *"What would you say about making a decision today — at least for what we've discussed and the budget we put together?"* or *"What would you say about going ahead and knowing that you made the decision to get started today?"*

You still may need to meet with them again with the final scope of services, but you will have obtained the formal commitment (and perhaps a deposit) to move forward.

3

# When?

## Future Or Past Events

Asking "when" seems like a pretty straightforward question that deals with timing — and it is.

However, there are several different types of "when" questions that you can ask to learn either the timing of future events or the history of those in the past.

A basic question concerning timing is *"When do you plan on getting started (letting us begin)?"* Here, you are asking for the timing of a decision.

It just as easily could be phrased *"When do you plan on making a decision on your new kitchen (other design or solution)?"*

While the two questions are similar, the second question actually is the more effective one because it supplies more information.

## Avoid Asking About "Time Frame"

The question *"What's your time frame?"* is such a poor question because it tells you nothing on its face.

I think we just copy it from others because we've heard them use it, but it is a totally worthless question. *Eliminate it.*

This is a poorly disguised "when" question that doesn't work.

If you ask someone what their "time frame" is, you may think you know what you mean by asking this question, but you should be asking when they can make a decision.

Similarly, your customers may think they know what they mean when they answer your question. However, they might have several different responses in mind.

As a result, you very likely will have a miscommunication because neither one of you is *exactly* sure what is meant by the question — and maybe even less sure after it has been answered.

You may think that you are asking your customers when they are prepared to make a decision by learning when they want to begin enjoying or using the solution you will be creating for them or when they want it installed or completed, but in order to learn this, you really need to ask specifically for the information you want and not use a more general question.

## It's The Decision Date That Matters

The *decision date* is the key to determining how you should work with a customer and how you structure your presentation.

*This is the question that you need to focus on and ask.*

Unless what you are selling can literally be purchased and then carried out of your establishment, delivered, installed, or commenced on the date of sale, when people plan on having or want to begin using your product or service doesn't usually equate with a decision date.

The dates could be days, weeks, months, or even years apart. What you must know is when they are capable of making a decision or how soon they intend to make it.

## The Fallacy Of "Time Frame"

In any case, "time frame" isn't a good or meaningful question to ask. The date when someone "needs" what you offer really isn't the issue.

What if "by the end of the year," "a year," "within a year," or "before the fall" is someone's "time frame" because they really don't "need" to have what you offer provided until then — but they can say "yes" to giving you the order, tendering the initial deposit or purchase order, and starting the paperwork *today*?

Then "time frame" is irrelevant from a sales standpoint.

Put another way, what have you really learned when your customers tell you that their "time frame" is "*July*" or "*October*" or some other time designation?

What if they tell you "*3 months,*" "*a few months,*" "*within the next year,*" "*in the spring,*" "*in the fall,*" "*before Christmas,*" "*before the holidays,*" "*after the holidays,*" "*by the end of the year,*" "*before school starts,*" "*as soon as school gets out,*" "*after the first of the year,*" "*next summer,*" or something similar?

Such responses really tell you nothing. You must ask additional questions to learn if and when a decision can be made.

## Don't Waste Your Questions

Why not be more specific from the beginning instead of asking a "throwaway" question like "time frame?"

If you're asking your customers about their "time frame," you're really asking a question that provides no clear answer to your question. Ask what you really want to know.

Your customers may think they know what you're asking when you talk about time frame and tell you what they think is an appropriate response, but you probably won't know what they mean by their answer without asking additional questions — because there are so many possible answers depending on how your customers interpret this question.

Therefore, avoid this question and ask for the specific information that you want.

## More Information Needed

To learn "when" your customers plan on doing something, you need to ask more than one question.

Just getting the decision date is not sufficient either because this doesn't answer all of your questions.

You need to know when they are capable of and prepared to make a decision, when they would like to have the work done, when they want it completed, and when they desire to begin using the new space or improvements you are discussing with them.

## There's No Time Like Today

Just because someone says that they intend to make a decision *"in a few weeks," "next month," "after the first of the year," "by the end of the year," "after their mother officially moves in with them,*" or some other non-specific future date doesn't necessarily mean that the decision has to wait that long.

*It could actually be made the day that you're asking the question — or the next day.* Doesn't *"within a year"* include *"today"*? Doesn't it include this week?

When a customer gives you this type of response, they are just indicating that they *think* that they are not close to making a decision. They really haven't focused on it yet or really determined what it will take for them to actually make the decision.

They may be more prepared to make a decision than they think, but you don't know just exactly what they think needs to happen before they can say "yes" to getting started with enjoying or using what you are offering.

Depending on what needs to happen before you can actually deliver your final proposal and get it approved by them, prepare their property for the work that needs to be done, secure the appropriate permissions and permits, and get started on the job, several months might elapse between now and then anyway.

That's why the decision can be made now — with the work being started at a later date. Therefore, get in the habit of asking questions that might reveal that a decision can be made much sooner than they thought.

## Learning About Pending Events

The "when" question can also help you learn about other pending events that need to be considered when asking your customers for a decision.

They help you clarify when they are expecting delivery of their baby (or grandbaby), when their son or daughter is graduating or returning from military service or getting married, when they think they will know for sure what they want in a product or service like you are recommending, when an important decision-maker or influencer will be available to look at or consider what you've been discussing with them, or when they might be available to meet with you again.

## Using Related Questions

As is true with the "who" and "what" questions, a "when" question can be asked using other styles and phrasing of questions that won't necessarily begin with the word "when" or have it in the question. For example, "what" needs to happen before they can make a decision is an indirect way of determining when it can happen.

Asking them to justify or explain their reasoning with a "why" question can serve as a "when" question — as in "why" they are waiting for a particular event to occur before making a decision or "why" they would want to put off a decision that seems appropriate to make now.

## Determining Future Contact Dates

"When" questions help you plan future contact.

Initially you'll want to talk by phone to everyone — or nearly everyone — after their initial conversation or presentation with you, and you'll want to determine when that will occur.

Usually you'll suggest a time, but you can ask your customers for their input in selecting the appropriate day or time for you to speak with them again.

There is absolutely nothing improper about asking your customers for their input for a future contact. Getting them involved in choosing what should happen next — or a date for it to happen — includes them in the process.

You don't necessarily have to agree with what they suggest — or the time or date — but this will give you a good idea of how receptive they are and how interested they might be in what you have to offer.

Rather than a sign of weakness, this interaction is quite strategic on your part.

## 4

# Where?

### Responses Tend To Be Factual

Unless you get a vague response like *"I don't know,"* *"I don't care,"* *"I'm not sure,"* *"It doesn't matter,"* or *"It depends,"* the "where" questions that you'll ask will tend to be more factual and have more specific responses than some of the other discovery questions.

The answers usually involve a definite physical location or a place (or occasionally a generalized area such "the kitchen" or "living room" without specifying what part of that room needs attention), and this generally will be somewhere inside their home although it could involve the garage, sidewalks, entrances, windows, exterior lighting, porches, stoops, roofing, siding, patios, decks, spas, or pools.

They will talk about an area within their home or on their property where they want the improvements made or the equipment installed or replaced.

## "Where' Questions Are Versatile

In addition to being factual (*"Where do you work now?"* or *"Where did you work before you retired?"* or *"Where did you live before moving here?"* or *"Where did you buy your car?"* or *"Where do your kids go to school?"* or *"Where do you want the tree planted?"*), "where" questions can reference a past event, indicate a preference, or point to a planned future event.

For instance, you can ask someone where they went on their vacation last summer, where they ate dinner last night, or where they went to college — all historical questions and responses.

You can ask people where they like to go to relax or unwind, where their favorite vacation spot is, or where they would like to go for a particular activity — questions about preferences.

You also can learn where people plan on going for the holidays or where they are going this weekend — questions and discussions about future events.

## Resources Used To Locate You

"Where" questions are useful for learning "how" people found out about you or located your office or showroom or "why" they are talking with you as a possible solution for their current need.

You can ask questions about where they saw your ad or message (and "why" they were looking there or "how often" they use that resource), where they heard about you (if it was from a friend, relative, or satisfied client), or where they typically look for information about the types of products or services you provide.

## Determining Preferences

To learn about preferences that will help you with trial closes or in selecting a specific product, design, or solution with your customers, you can use various "where" questions to ask about how they intend to use what you are proposing or discussing with them.

For instance, ask your customers where they need specific help. Pin it down to an exact location in their home or yard.

## Using "Nesting"

An emotional selling technique that causes your customers to visualize using and actually owning what you are showing or discussing with them is called *"nesting."* This lets them feel like they are already own and are using and benefitting from what you are offering them.

Without any overt pressure or direction from you, it makes agreeing to purchase from you easier since they have already assumed ownership.

They have begun to "see" how your solution will address the needs that they have and will not want to have you leave without agreeing for you to provide it.

If it is an actual product or device you are suggesting as part of your overall solution, you might even leave it for a day or two for them to experience it. This is an example of the "puppy-dog close" where they get so attached to what you left them and enjoy using it — as if they already purchased it — that they won't let you take it back, and you will have made a sale.

If it is a custom order or something you need to fabricate or design, help them visualize where it will be and how it will perform. Walk them through it, or use a PowerPoint or video to help them experience it.

If it's new space that you are creating or offering, ask them how they would use it and get them to share with you where various piece of furniture, equipment, or fixtures would be located.

Help them to experience how much better your solution will be for them than what they have now.

## Personalization

Get your customers involved in owning what you are showing them by asking them if they can live with or accept the design as it is or where they would want or need to make any additions or changes to what you have described or illustrated to make it even better for their needs.

Determine where your customers would like to make any upgrades to turn the product or construction solution you are proposing into the perfect solution for them and get them closer to an ownership decision.

Such changes, modifications, custom features, upgrades, or upsells could include flooring, styling, cabinetry, hardware, furniture, colors, styles, size or capacity, storage, drawers, doors, materials, weight, security, energy efficiency, appliances, fixtures, terms, lighting, warranty, trim, accents, accessories, or similar treatments — depending on the service or product involved.

Find out where they want your product or service to be as unique or personal to them as possible, and build your trial closes around that.

## Making The Decision

A great question that transcends historical, preference, and future perspectives of the "where" question is the one that learns where they are in making a decision.

This question asks *"Where are you in your thought process as far as deciding on what we have talked about?"* or

*"Where do you (you folks) stand as far as making a decision on getting started with your remodeling?"* or *"Where do you think you are as far as making up your mind (minds) on letting us get started with your remodeling (construction, renovation)?"* or *"Where do you think you are as far as deciding which plan (proposal, solution, design) to pursue?"*

Then you can work with the answers to these questions to continue building the sale.

"Where" indicates a strong interest by identifying a specific location for the improvements, and it precedes the actual decision.

Once you know the "what" and the "where," you can make the sale or get the order.

# 5

# Why?

## The Most Basic Question

"Why?" is a very common question.

Children learn very early in life to question anything going on around them that they don't understand, and usually *"why"* is an inherent part of their questions.

"Why" is reflexive. It can stand by itself as a total question. It can be used in conjunction with most other discovery questions, and it can be an add-on to any question.

## Don't Overuse

"Why" questions are great when you want to learn about someone's motivation for thinking about a service or product such as you offer, what they're thinking, how deeply they hold an attitude or opinion, or when you require additional information or insight about what you are discussing with them — but be careful.

"Why" questions easily can be overdone and become very tedious and boring. You literally — like a small child — can ask "why" after almost anything that is said by your customers.

Some people can't or don't want to verbalize their rationale or thinking about a particular product, service, design, or solution that you might be discussing with them or that they might be considering or looking at in your showroom or warehouse.

Rather than opening up about their opinions and sharing them with you, they can become defensive.

## "Why" — In Other Words

As with other discovery questions, you can vary the wording you use to elicit an explanation — in addition to the ones where you specifically start the question with the word "why" or use the word "why" as part of your question.

Certainly you can ask "*Why do you feel that way?*" or "*Why is that?*" or "*Can you tell me why?*"

However, you can also use "*Would you please explain?*" or "*I don't think I understand,*" or "*I'm not sure what you mean by that,*" or "*Could you please elaborate?*"

Your customers just need to understand and appreciate that you're asking them for more information or an explanation or elaboration of what they've just said or expressed.

Often, an *"Oh?"* or *"Really?"* — or a surprised or questioning look or expression by you (such as raised eyebrows, a quizzical look, a slightly open mouth, or a tilt of your head) after their comment — will serve the same purpose as asking a "why" question.

The important part of using a "why" or "why"-type question is that you get people to give you more information to support or explain their response, opinion, reasoning, feelings, or logic.

## Motivating Influences

In addition to asking introductory discovery questions like *"Why are you thinking of (planning on) getting a kitchen makeover (room addition, porch enclosure, or other type of solution or renovation)?"* or *"Why did you decide to contact me today?"* there are many other "why," "why not," and "why"-type questions that you can use — to learn about someone's motivation and interest in seeking a product, solution, or design such as you offer.

Often, one "why" question will lead to another "why" question — or a "how" or "what," for instance — for an explanation or clarification.

You can ask someone why they chose the home, layout, or floor plan they have now, or why they believe or feel it no longer meets their current needs.

You can ask why they have chosen this particular time (in general or specifically this day) to look for an answer to their perceived or expressed needs, or why they identified you to visit or contact and consider working with for that solution, design, product, or service.

## **Experiences In The Marketplace**

To gain an understanding of what people have experienced in the marketplace or online before deciding to contact or visit you, learn what they have been looking at with other companies or on various websites and why they determined that their needs couldn't be met at those other places or companies.

"Why" questions get to the heart of what someone is looking for and how well they think it meets their needs. It allows you to compare other things they have seen and considered with what you offer and determine their opinions and preferences.

Perhaps they have been disappointed with what they have seen on their own, they are just getting started in their search, or they have not found anything within their budget. It could be a reluctance to make a decision or a basic fear of making a change from what they have now.

This is where you can help provide direction and shore up their confidence. Sometimes living with a poor situation seems easier than making a change.

## Measuring Preferences

"Why" questions are great for learning attitudinal or lifestyle preferences — such as why they like or dislike something you are showing them or why they prefer or think they want something they saw (at a competitor's showroom, on TV, online, or elsewhere).

You can determine why certain features or design elements are important for them to have while others are not. Asking "why" questions can help you eliminate various designs, layouts. and features from consideration.

When your customers don't like certain plans that you have shown them, discussed with them, or want to show them, you can focus on helping them select something else that is more in keeping with what they are trying to accomplish.

## Clarifying Other Issues

"Why" questions can help provide answers, explanations, opinions, and attitudes concerning other parts of your presentation.

For instance, as you begin your presentation you learn

who all of the people are in the customer unit that are present with you, but then you might discover that at least one family member, decision-maker, or influencer who needs to be present is absent.

From that, you can attempt to learn why the influencers or other members are missing from the presentation or what prevented them from being present — and if they are likely to be present at a future meeting.

You also can learn why someone needs to be consulted, what they can contribute to the process, what their thought process is, and how their input or influence will affect your customer's decision.

If a decision is going to be delayed, you're going to want to know why this is the case also.

## **Facilitating The Close**

When you narrow their search to just a specific product, service, design, or solution — and they seem quite interested in pursuing it with you — you can reinforce their interest and excitement level by exploring what they like about your proposed solution and why they think it works so well for them.

You especially want to learn why they feel it meets their needs better than or to the exclusion of everything else they have seen. This will produce a trial close.

When you ask your final closing question, and it doesn't produce a buying decision, you may need to ask what it will take or what needs to happen (and why) before they can make their decision.

## Teaming Up With Other Questions

You'll find that a strategically asked "why" or "why"-type question will work with any of your other discovery questions.

While the "who," "what," "when," "where," "how," and "which" questions also are important to your discovery, well-timed "why" questions can go right along with them to help you understand the reasoning and the emotions behind the answers more fully and completely.

Often, the "why" will provide the necessary insight to explain answers to other questions.

## Working With Objections

"Why" is a great question to use when your customers raise objections or issues — about something you're showing them or for not going ahead with a decision that seems to already be made.

In addition to finding out what the issue or concern is that they are raising, you can ask them why this issue is a concern, why they hold that opinion, or why they feel this way — and you can learn how strongly they hold that opinion or viewpoint.

When people want to "think about" what you've presented to them, they try to put off making a decision altogether, or they give you some other reason for not proceeding, you can ask them why they would need more time. Then you can help them clarify the reasons why they should make a decision now.

As you review with them all of the reasons why they liked what you were showing them and how this meets and solves the needs they've expressed, you can ask them why they would want to wait and possibly miss out on an opportunity that is ready for them to act on right now.

6

# How?

## Measuring An Amount Or Opinion

The "how" and the related "how much," "how soon," "how long," and "how often" questions request mostly factual or quantitative information from your customers — even if it's just an educated guess on their part.

"How" and "how"-type questions may also call for an opinion or explanation, or you can use "how" or related questions such as "how well," "how much," "how strongly" or "how important" questions to measure attitudes, acceptance, or preferences.

You might want to know the degree of certainty or conviction that someone has about a particular position or belief — or how plausible something might seem to them.

For instance, you could ask, *"How important is it for you to have …?"* or *"How do (would) you feel about …?"* or

"How about ...?" or "How strongly do you feel about ...?" or "How would (does) this work for you?"

## An Introductory Question

The "how" question is one of the first that you will ask in your initial discovery with a new customer — whether it's a phone conversation or a visit to your office, showroom, warehouse, or display.

You will want to know how they heard about or learned about you or your company.

After greeting your customers, introducing yourself, and learning who they are, you'll ask a beginning question such as *"How did you hear (learn) about us (me)?"* or *"How did you happen to hear (learn) about us (me, our products, our services)?"*

## "How" Leads To Other Questions

After your customers tell you how they learned about or heard about you, you'll want to know more. While you're interested in the factual answer to your question — website, newspaper ad, sign, friend, or some other source — you are interested in learning why that source was used.

You also want to know how important or influential that source was in prompting their visit or contact, what specifically it was in your message that caused them to decide to visit or call you, and if they also used other sources besides the ones they mentioned to learn about you and what you offer.

If they say that they visited your website, then you'll want to learn more about how that happened — *"How did you learn about our website?"* or *"Do you remember what you saw on our website that stood out as important to you?"*

## Learning About Their Online Search

If you determine that they learned about what you offer or found you online, you can ask "how" they conducted their online search, which search engines they may have used, and what key words or phrase they used with *"How did you search for our site or happen to locate it?"* or *"What phrase (key words) did you use for your search when you found our website?"* or *"What site did you start with to link to (find) us?"* *"Do you remember what search terms or phrase you used that led you to our (my) site?"*

You'll also want to know if they used anything else in addition to your website to learn about and locate you — a sign, one of your ads, or talking with someone who has visited or worked with you in some capacity.

## Finding Out About Other Sources

If they answer that they saw a newspaper or print ad, you can ask *"What in particular in the ad caught your attention (was important to you)?"* or *"Do you remember what stood out in our ad that caught (attracted) your attention (eye)?"* or *"What did you notice as being important to you that was in our ad?"*

What you're trying to learn is how important the ad was in connecting with them or in prompting their visit.

There may be other aspects of your print ad that you'll also want to ask about, such as the day they saw it, if they've seen any of your other ads (and where and when — as well as what the ads may have featured, if they recall), and how often they look at that publication for products, services, or solutions.

Similar types of "how" questions can be used for other sources that people may have used, such as radio, TV, or signage.

You can ask *"What in particular in the commercial caught your attention (was important to you)?"* or *"Do you remember what stood out in our commercial that caught (attracted) your attention (eye, interest)?"* or *"Do you remember where you saw our sign?"* or *"Do you remember what the sign depicted that attracted your interest?"*

When a friend, relative, or acquaintance told them about you, ask *"What specifically did your friend tell you about me (us) that prompted you to contact me?"* or *"Have they used our services in the past?"*

## Questions Are Interchangeable

Asking someone about how they located or learned about you does double-duty. It explains which source or sources they used to locate or learn about you prior to visiting or contacting you, and it provides a reason why they have chosen to contact you at this time – or an opportunity for you to learn this.

It may also tell you or indicate what is important for your customers to find in a product, service, or solution, such as the design, capacity, size, warranty, features, pricing, or financing.

By now, you should appreciate the inter-relationship of questions and that there often are several ways of asking for similar or essentially the same type of information.

## Indicating Preferences And Intent

After discussing some available choices, products, services, concepts, or solutions, you can ask your customers questions about how well what you have described or illustrated meets their needs to determine how you want to proceed.

"How" questions make great trial closing questions –and even transition into the final close – because they invite a qualitative response or ask for a preference among various choices or options.

For instance, "*How does this design work for you?*" or "*How do you feel about this particular product or solution?*" or "*What do you think of this design (plan, idea)?*" or "*How does this compare to what you have now (are currently using, had in mind)?*" or "*How well does this design (approach, product, or solution) solve (address or eliminate) the issues that you're dealing with (facing, concerned about)?*"

You could also ask "nesting," preference, or utilization questions during your presentation, such as "*How would you rearrange your furniture in this space after we complete the renovation?*" or "*How many steps do you think this design (product or solution) will save you (you and others in your home) in a typical day?*" or "*How much safer do you think you will be with this this concept (solution, design, product)?*"

## Creating Tie-Downs

You can expand your use of the "how" and "how"-type questions to help you illustrate specific aspects of what you are showing and cause your customers to become more emotionally attached to those products, services, or solutions.

You might ask questions such as "*How much more convenient would it be to have (what you are describing)*" or "*Can you imagine how much easier it will be with a design (solution, product) such as this?*"

## Of Degrees And Amounts

"How" questions are useful for getting opinions, but they also are great for creating contrasts, providing comparisons, or asking rhetorical questions.

They help get your customers to project or imagine how they might use certain features or aspects of what you are showing them — or to consider comfort and convenience facets of your product or solution.

## Measuring With "How Much"

"How much" questions are good to use when you are looking for a time or usage response — or an amount of money.

Ask your customers about how much time they have for your presentation, how long they had planned (for the length of your presentation) on meeting with you today, how much of an investment they are looking for or considering, how much they intend to finance on their new purchase, or how much of a hurry they are in to find a solution and get it installed or implemented.

## Learning Timing With "How Soon"

There also are "how soon" questions that allow you to gauge a time component for a future event from your customers.

Learn how soon they want to act, how soon they are prepared to make a decision and get started, or how soon they need to have a solution in place — as well as others that give you a time perspective.

## Using "How Long" To Focus

The "how long" question is related to the "how soon" question and can be used interchangeably with it to measure time.

You can ask your customers how long before they'll know specifically what they want in a design, layout, product, solution, redesign, or renovation — or how long they have been considering having something done to alleviate or address their issues.

Similarly, you can ask how long (how much time) they have for your initial presentation, or how long (how much longer) they are willing to go on using, settling for, or putting up with a product, design, space, or situation that no longer meets their needs.

## Making Direct Comparisons

"How" questions — even if they don't begin with the word "how" — are useful for making direct comparisons.

You can ask questions beginning with "how" or you can ask your customers to "compare" or "contrast" a floor plan, layout, design, product, idea, feature, or solution that you're presenting to them with something else they've seen, experienced, thought about, or imagined.

This could involve what they've seen on the internet or TV, what they have now, what they have looked at or discussed with someone else, or what you are showing them.

When you show a *specific* product, service, solution, or opportunity for them to consider, you can ask how they think this can meet their needs better than anything else you've discussed with them or anything that they have seen on their own.

Learn how what you're showing them — as you've narrowed it down to something they can actually decide to purchase or lease — compares with what they thought they would see or what might be available, how it compares to what they currently have, how it compares to what they have determined they need in a new product or solution, or how well it satisfies what they need to have in a product, service, or solution.

## Forming Conclusions

"How" and "how"-type questions can cause your customers to focus on why something is important to them, explain how they might use the product or service you are presenting to them, or justify certain features they want to have.

"How" questions help reinforce aspects of your presentation by causing your customers to focus on specific features or benefits.

"How" questions help you learn if something is important to your customers — and the degree of importance or emphasis that they place on it.

They allow your customers to explain why they like or dislike something.

"How" questions really get to the core of making a sale or obtaining an agreement to proceed.

# 7

# Which?

## The Ultimate Choice Question

"Which" is a great question because it calls for a conclusion — a decision. When used correctly, there is no doubt that you're asking someone about their preference, choice, or selection.

For instance, *"Which one do you like, 'A' or 'B'?"* or *"Which one do you prefer?"* or *"Which one would you like to have us install?"* or *"Which one have you selected?"* or *"Which one have you decided on?"*

## Don't Force It

You should only ask for a decision or a selection — a "which one" choice — after you have given your customers some specific examples or you know that they have enough information to be able to answer your question rather than just asking for a general preference.

If there is any concern that someone is confused or has not made up their mind on a layout, design, feature, color, or style that you have shown them — or that it is unlikely that they can express their opinion or choice — the "which" question won't give you a specific answer.

In that case, go for a little clarification, as in *"Which one are you leaning toward?"* or *"Which one do you think you prefer?"* or *"If you had to make a choice, which one do you feel the strongest (best) about?"* or *"If we had to eliminate any from consideration, which one do you think you we should remove (get rid of, set aside)?"* Even here, you may not get a definitive response.

## Reflexive Questions

Asking a "which" question should get almost an automatic response — one that people don't have to pause and think about too much before they answer.

To get your customers used to answering either a specific choice question or a recall question — and to find out how well they can respond to a "which" question — you can give them a couple of easy ones in the beginning of your presentation.

Set up a little test to determine if they are comfortable answering "which" or "which"-type questions. For instance, in the early part of your conversation with someone — on the telephone, at their home, or in your office or showroom — you might ask *"Which newspaper did you see our ad in?"* or *"Which day was that?"* or *"Which search engine did you use to find our website?"*

Here you'll get either a specific response, or an *"I don't know,"* or *"I don't remember,"* or *"I'm not sure."* When they say that they don't remember — or they don't appear to try very hard to remember — this might signal a general low level of interest in finding a solution, in working with you, or in being able to make any type of decision.

It also could mean that they really don't remember, that it didn't matter that much to them for them to make a point of specifically remembering it, or that they aren't very good at remembering details.

Nevertheless, there is no right or wrong, or good or bad answer to a "which" question — you're only asking for information and for people to reveal a preference, choice, or selection.

Be alert to the possibility that they aren't serious, however, if you get a weak or noncommittal response to your questions.

## Getting Market Information

"Which" questions can help you learn about your marketplace and what your customers have focused on in it. It may give you information on your competition also.

For instance, you can ask someone about what else they have seen, looked at, or considered with *"Have you talked with any other companies or visited any other showrooms?"* or *"Which products (solutions, designs) have you been concentrating on looking at to help you arrive at a decision?"* or *"Which ideas from what you have seen online (on the internet) seem to appeal to you the most?"*

These questions are asked as much to help you learn about your marketplace and competition — as well as online shopping opportunities — and what people find important or comparable to what you are offering as they are to help you focus on working with a specific customer.

## Asking The Closing Question

The "which" questions — above all the others you can ask — lead to the actual final decision because they indicate actually making a choice and beginning ownership of the solution that is being presented.

This is a definitive question that calls for a decision, such as *"Which one (product, layout, design, color, style, model, size) do you prefer?"* or *"Of what we have looked at today, which one (product, layout, design, color, style, model, size) do you think you would like to own?"* or *"Which of these 2 (3) plans (layouts, designs, colors, styles, models, sizes) that we've looked at today (so far, this week) is the one you'd like to own?"* or *"Which one would you like to own (have installed, delivered)?"*

Once that question is answered, you can proceed to the final closing question.

## Setting Up Trial Closes

As you narrow your focus on "which" plan, design, layout, solution, style, color, model, or brand your customers would like to own, there are various choices that you can ask them to make as trial closing questions.

These questions help your customers identify with the products or solutions you're showing them, cause them to visualize it as being their own, and make it possible to close on the entire sale eventually.

As long as they are making choices, they are becoming more involved with owning what you are showing and discussing with them.

You can clarify colors, accessories, accents, trim, styles, hardware, packages, fixtures, and other features — included or optional — realizing that these can be easily added or removed to make the sale and stay within a budgeted amount.

## Asking "Which" In Other Ways

As with other types of discovery questions, "which" and "which"-type questions don't always need the word "which" in them.

For instance, *"How do you feel about …?"* or *"Do you want a …?"* are just other ways of asking *"Which style (features, layout, design) do you like (want, prefer)?"* or *"Which one appeals to you?"* or *"Do you like (prefer, want, favor) this one or the other one we just looked at?"*

Another important series of "which" questions focus on which type of financing or payment option they want to use, which form of payment they desire, or which funding sources are available to them or appropriate for them to use.

# 8

# More Questions

## Other Possibilities

So far in this book, I have been focusing on having you ask questions to elicit information from your customers by using the "who," "what," "when," "where," "why," "how," and "which" types of questions — whether the questions actually begin with those words, have those words somewhere in the questions, or are phrased in a way that you will obtain such information in the responses.

These are solid question formats that will serve you quite well and enable you to form a complete picture of your customers as you learn about their needs and build the sale.

However, there are a few other ways of asking questions that I want you to be aware of to give you additional discovery possibilities.

## Yes/No Questions

We have all used "yes/no" questions throughout our lives. We have been asked such questions, and we have asked others these questions.

They are very conversational and come to us rather easily.

They definitely have a place in the sales interview — especially when you just need a confirmation or agreement.

However, if you need a more complete response, a short answer, or an explanation, the "yes/no" format is not recommended.

There will be times when you might just need a quick "yes" or "no" without any elaboration or explanation — depending on how you have phrased your question — to be able to continue with your presentation or move on to something else.

There are many examples of "yes/no" questions that you can use. Some will totally stand alone. Some will be a lead-in to other questions.

Examples of standalone questions — where just the "yes" or "no" answer will suffice — are ones like "*Is it still raining outside?*" or "*Are they still working on Route 7?*" or "*Do you have time for me to show you …?*" or "*Would *you like a glass of water?"* or *"Would you care to sit down?"*

Such types of questions can be more conversational — especially at the beginning — than specifically part of your presentation.

## Trial Closing Or Selection Questions

Even in the selection process or as trial closes, "yes/no" questions can be used when both you and the customer know what the answer is revealing.

They are great to get your customers to indicate a preference when it's just a matter of whether they like, prefer, or want something or they don't — no other choices. This is just a simply matter of "yes" they like something or want it — or "no" they don't.

Occasionally, you may get a *"We're not sure,"* or *"Possibly,"* or *"It depends."* This means the "yes/no" question was not an effective type of question in this instance.

Obviously, you will need to ask more questions to shed some light on the ambiguity or to give you some more information on where to go with your presentation.

Sometimes — even though a "yes" or "no" can answer the question — you will get a more complete response to your question. They may answer *"yes"* or *"no"* and then proceed to defend their answer or tell you why this is the case. That's fine.

## Questions That Lead To Another

Sometimes the "yes/no" question can be used for variety in the types of questions you ask or how you phrase them — or as a lead-in to a "who," "what," "when," "where," "why," "how," or "which" type of question.

When you are beginning your presentation, you might ask someone if they saw your newspaper ad or visited your website. Regardless of whether they say "yes," "no," or they aren't sure, you want more information, so you'll explore their response with additional questions.

You can use a "yes/no" question during your presentation for confirmation of something you are suggesting. At other times, you will likely need to ask more specific questions than "yes" or "no" to determine exactly what they prefer and want to own in the solution you are proposing.

## Use This Tool Appropriately

The "yes/no" questions can be effective when you need a quick preference answer, a verification, or you don't require a longer explanation.

Just be careful not to use them too often.

The real heart of your discovery is still your "who," "what," "when," "where," "why," "how," and "which" types of questions. If you use the "yes/no" too often, it may become tedious.

"Yes/no" questions can't completely reveal how prepared they are to make a decision or how well they think what you are showing them can serve their needs.

## Scaling Questions For Opinions

Another type or style of question that you can use is the scaling or rating question where you ask people to compare or contrast something you are showing them with their idea of the "perfect" product or solution for them.

In this type of question, the lower the rating the more disinterested or dissatisfied people are with something you are discussing with them. A higher number means that they are closer to accepting the premise you are offering them.

This can be a great trial closing question, but there is one significant drawback.

## Scaling Question Limitations

Many people simply cannot express their feelings in a ranked, comparative, or quantified response so it may have limited usefulness as a questioning technique —

depending on the specific customers you are working with at the time.

Some people tend to respond with something toward the middle — regardless of what you are asking. If they really like something, they may only give you a "6" or a "7" in response. They may stick with just the "4-6" range to express "average" and let it go at that.

Then you'll have to try to interpret what they mean by asking them additional questions.

Some people are more absolute and definite in their responses — giving you a "1" or even a "0" if they really don't like it and a "9" or "10" if they are impressed.

Some tend to overanalyze their response and vacillate between a few numbers — not really picking anything.

Others just don't like to commit themselves and will say that they are not very good at coming up with a number or answer your question with a non-numeric answer, such as *"pretty good"* or *"not bad."*

This is why the scaling or rating questions are not always that good to use.

Often, when several people are involved in the decision, you'll get rankings that are vastly different — with some people liking your idea a lot while others are not in support.

## Examples Of Scaling Questions

Scaling questions ask people to compare or contrast something against, or in terms of, their "ideal." This only works if they have a good idea of what they're looking for and are able to express that on a 1-10 scale. Then you'll have something to build on.

Still, you are attempting to quantify objectively what is a totally subjective issue. That in itself presents challenges because there is no standard to apply to the rankings.

You might ask *"On a scale of 1-10, how well does this product (plan, design, solution, idea, concept, space) meet your needs?"* or *"On a scale of 1-10, how would you rate this as the ideal plan (design, solution, product, idea, concept, space) for you?"* or *"On a scale of 1-10, with 10 being the absolute best, how do you rate this solution as being what you're looking for (what you need)?"* or *"On a scale of 1-10, with 10 being the highest, rate this concept (design, solution, idea, product, style, size, concept, space) for me as far as being what you've been looking for?"*

Then you can focus on any responses less than a "9" or "10" with questions such as *"What would it need to have to go from the '7' you're giving it now to a '9' or a '10'?"* or *"What would this need to have to make it a '9' or a '10' instead of the '7' you are giving it now?"* *"Why do you give it just a '7' or an '8' — what is missing (needed)?"*

or *"Only a '6' — it seemed like you really liked this plan (design, product, solution, idea, style, concept, space)?"*

The scaling question should only be used once or twice in a presentation as a serious trial closing question. It is another way of asking *"How well does this plan (design, solution, product, concept, idea, style, space) work for you?"* or *"How do you feel about owning (going ahead with) this product (plan, design, solution, idea, concept, space)?"* or *"How does this compare to what you had in mind?"* or *"Is this the one you want to own (have us do for you, have us get started on))?"*

Then you can address their response and continue with your presentation. You might have a sale at that point, or you might back at the beginning — asking more questions.

## Using Scaling Questions To Clarify

In addition to learning how well your customers may like something you're showing them — presumably as a trial closing question that is a preliminary one to the final closing question — you may get information that suggests that you need to regroup and change what you are showing them.

Scaling questions can give you terrific feedback so that you'll know if something important is missing or if you have misread what they are looking for. Possibly their opinions of what they wanted or needed have changed a little as they have experienced what you have been showing or describing to them.

You need to clarify what they like in what you have been showing them and what is missing or what changes they would like to see.

Get them to elaborate on how or why something is not what they are looking for or what they want. The scaling question may be a great way to get them to assess how well they like something or feel that it is the ideal solution for their needs by quantifying their response.

Just be careful not to overuse this technique.

## Alternate- Choice Questions

In addition to asking "yes/no" or scaling questions to learn preferences, you can gather information and employ trial closes with a questioning technique called "alternate-choice."

Essentially you will be giving your customers two choices to select from — one of which you are reasonably certain they will select.

The key is just using two choices. Don't try this as an open-ended question or as a multiple-choice. This is an alternate-choice — between just two possibilities. They are to pick one of the two.

You can ask your customer if it's important for them to have a certain feature in a product you are describing or thinking of showing them — and get a "yes." "no," or "possibly" — or you can frame it differently to learn more about what is important to them and what they are seeking.

You could use an alternate-choice question and explain that you can show them something with two distinct and separate features or treatments that they want or the same idea or product that combines those two features into one. Then you ask *"Which would you prefer?"*

This technique is useful when you have two or more choices of a color, style, approach, concept, design, version or other variations where the basic product or solution is not affected — just the price and utility to your customer. That's why you ask for their choice.

Be careful that you don't ask for a choice before you have given them enough information to make an intelligent selection or for you to understand their needs well enough to frame those choices properly.

It could even be a case of offering someone the choice of taking delivery on something that you have in inventory that you'd really like to sell — that is not exactly what they requested but close to it where you can offer it at a better price than one they would have to wait for until after you ordered it.

## Getting A Definitive Answer

It's possible that when you ask your customers for a choice between two design concepts, layouts, included features, colors, sizes, or styles that they will ask you if that is all that is available or if they could pick something else as a custom design or upgrade.

This is a great trial closing technique and will allow you to secure agreement on what they really want — subject to budgetary constraints and the overall remodeling objective.

## Versatility Of This Technique

The alternate-choice question is a good one to intersperse in your sales interview and conversation to add variety and versatility to your trial closing questions.

It can indicate a preference more definitively than a "yes" or "no" response.

The alternate-choice does the work of a "which one" question or a "what" question — giving you the flexibility to ask questions in different ways.

## The Probe

In Chapter 5, I mentioned using a raised eyebrow, a surprised or quizzical look, or an *"Oh?"* or *"Really?"* to get your customer to elaborate on what they were telling you — a variation on asking *"why?"*

Even a pause with your hand cupped around your chin — or stroking your chin — and a puzzled *"Hmmm"* can elicit an explanation.

A probe is any type of question — like these or even any of the other "who," "what," "when," "where," "why," "how," and "which" questions — where you ask for a clarification or additional information.

Other examples are *"Tell me more,"* or *"Can you elaborate?"* or *"Can you please explain what you mean?"* or *"How's that?"* or *"I don't understand,"* or *"Can you be more specific?"* or *"Can you give me an example of that (what you mean)?"* or *"What makes you say that?"* or *"Help me understand,"* or *"I'm not following you,"* or *"Not sure exactly what you mean (by that),"* or *"Can you be more specific?"* or *"Care to explain?"* or *"That's interesting,"* or *"Interesting that you would (should) say that."*

## The Porcupine

Sometimes you won't be the one asking the questions. You'll be on the receiving end temporarily. Think of a porcupine, a pineapple, or a cactus — not something you'd want to have someone throw and expect you to catch. It's sharp and prickly.

# More Questions

So, if someone were to throw you some thorny object like this — and you had to catch it — what would be your first inclination? You'd want to catch it as lightly as possible and to get rid of it immediately. You wouldn't want to hang onto it.

Keep this concept in mind for addressing many questions that you get. I'm not talking about factual ones, such as when your customers ask what color something comes in or how much a particular feature is.

Rather, use this porcupine technique as a type of probe to send the question back to your customers with a question of your own.

Maybe you've heard or been told to answer a question with a question? That's what this technique is all about.

However, you need to use this form of questioning strategically, or it will seem trite, insincere, and overworked.

If someone asks if they can get a particular design, style, color, feature, finish, or trim — possibly something you haven't discussed with them or offered in the conversation — and you allow it, just answer the question affirmatively and confirm that this would be a choice they would select for their new product Then make a note on your information card or tablet and continue with your presentation.

## Answering Objections

Use the porcupine technique for clarification of an objection or concern that your customers might raise or ask about.

For instance, they might say something like *"Why is this only available in red?"* or *"This item (product, concept) seems pretty small,"* or *"Why are your services so expensive?"* Before you can even begin to answer their question, you need to know more about why they have asked this.

You can use a probe by expressing that you're not sure what they mean by their question or asking them to elaborate on their comments or to explain their concerns.

You also can toss the question back to them with a puzzled *"Why is this only available in red?"* or *"Just in red?"* or *"Red?"* to learn why they have asked this.

## The "Troll"

Beware of the "troll."

This is a tricky type of question that people might ask you. It's a trap so be careful.

"Troll" is a word I created to apply to this type or form of question — adapted from a similar meaning in online chats, forums, and comments. It's not a legitimate question, but you can easily add credence to it by the way you answer it.

It begins with a premise that something is universal, when in fact, it is not. It may only be their opinion, an urban legend, or conventional wisdom. However, if you allow the premise to stand by addressing the second part of their question, you have agreed to the first part.

Someone may start with an inclusive statement like *"Everyone knows that contractors (name of other group or profession) are in trouble,"* or *"Everyone knows that companies have plenty of room to negotiate,"* or *"Everyone knows that all list prices are subject to negotiation."* Then they'll explain why you're not competitive or why they are entitled to a big concession.

They might also say or imply something else that sounds like a universal statement — but is without merit.

## Avoid Taking The Bait

Rather than taking the bait about "everyone knows" or "all contractors," just ask *"Why do you say that?"* or *"What makes you say that?"* or *"Really?"* or *"Based on what?"*

Make them defend their position or explain what they are trying to accomplish by making such a statement. Then, you can work with their concern from a more factual or issue-oriented standpoint.

Also, be careful in trying to distance or differentiate your company from your competition by saying that you're not like all of the other companies or that you're different than the others.

You won't have uncovered the reason they made the statement, and you could get deeper into discussing — or even arguing about — their claim instead of addressing their real concern or issue constructively.

Strip away the generalizations and ask questions to determine what they are looking for and how ready, willing, and able they are to make a decision.

# 9

# Go Discover

## Summary Of Question Choices

In this book, I've given you the basics of discovery — the art of getting to know who you're working with in any sales or remodeling encounter and how to determine their basic needs and requirements.

This includes people walking into your office or showroom, those calling for information on the phone, those sending in a third part-party surrogate to meet with you and gather information, and those who contact you by email — directly or through your website.

You start with just the introduction and go from there.

With the various questioning strategies that I've illustrated, you can learn who the various people are that are participating in the decision, what needs to happen before the decision can occur, where people are in their search process, how people located you and what their expectations are, how to determine what's important to your customers, trial closing questions that you can use to help in the selection process, and the final close that signifies ownership.

You can create relationships with your customers and potential customers — more than anything else, sales are built upon and result from strong relationships.

## The Inter-Relationship Of Questions

As I took you through each chapter — who, what, when, where, why, how, and which (plus the additional types of questions) — I illustrated for you how many of the questions are inter-related and how there are various ways of asking for essentially the same information.

This way, you can vary your techniques and questioning style and use what's comfortable for you and your customers.

You can keep your discovery interview with your customers fresh, and somewhat spontaneous.

You can ask someone when they would like to start using their new product or solution, when they intend to make a decision or will be able to do so, what needs to happen before they can make a decision, or how soon they would like to have your design or solution created or installed.

These are all various ways of getting essentially the same information or confirming responses from other questions.

## Keep The Questions Interesting

By having many different ways of asking the same basic question — or for requesting essentially the same information — you can vary the way you ask your questions.

Even with the same customer, you can ask for the same information in various ways — in case the first answer seemed incomplete or vague — or you want to verify that what they told you earlier in the presentation is still true later.

Don't feel that you need to follow a certain regimen by starting with "who" questions and going through the other types of questions we've discussed — in order.

Your presentation will develop a certain rhythm and style. There will be questions that you'll typically ask your customers at the outset of your presentation to learn who they are and what they want to accomplish, but the rest will depend on their needs, interest level, and ability to act.

## So Now What?

I've given you a strategic approach to asking questions.

I've included a variety of questions and various ways to ask a similar question.

Don't feel that this is a comprehensive list of questions or that you need to adhere to these — I want you to inject your own personality and style.

They are provided as a guideline and to help you be aware of the many ways of involving your customers in the conversations you are having and the presentations you are conducting.

Besides, there will be issues raised during your presentation or your post-contact follow-up that will evoke and require their own specific questions.

By using questions such as I have provided here, you'll have a great start at building a successful sales presentation, connecting with your customers, and being a more effective contractor or aging-in-place solutions provider.

# Steve Hoffacker

**Steve Hoffacker**, CAPS, MCSP, MIRM, is principal of Hoffacker Associates LLC, a sales training (new home sales, universal design, and aging-in-place) and coaching company based in West Palm Beach, Florida.

Steve is an award-winning, internationally-recognized and experienced new home salesperson and sales trainer, as well as a universal design/aging-in-place safety and accessibility sales trainer and instructor.

For more than 30 years, he has helped homebuilders, new home salespeople, contractors and remodelers, new home marketers, designers, architects, occupational therapists, and other professionals to be more visible, competitive, profitable, and effective — and to really enjoy themselves as they pursue their business and create wonderful customer experiences.

Steve wants you and your company to be successful and has created this guide (and many others) to help make that happen.

This book will be a great resource to help you take your business to another level and outpace the competition.

Use these strategies and concepts for your professional success.

www.ingramcontent.com/pod-product-compliance
Lightning Source LLC
Chambersburg PA
CBHW070817100426
**42742CB00012B/2387**